ROOM 30

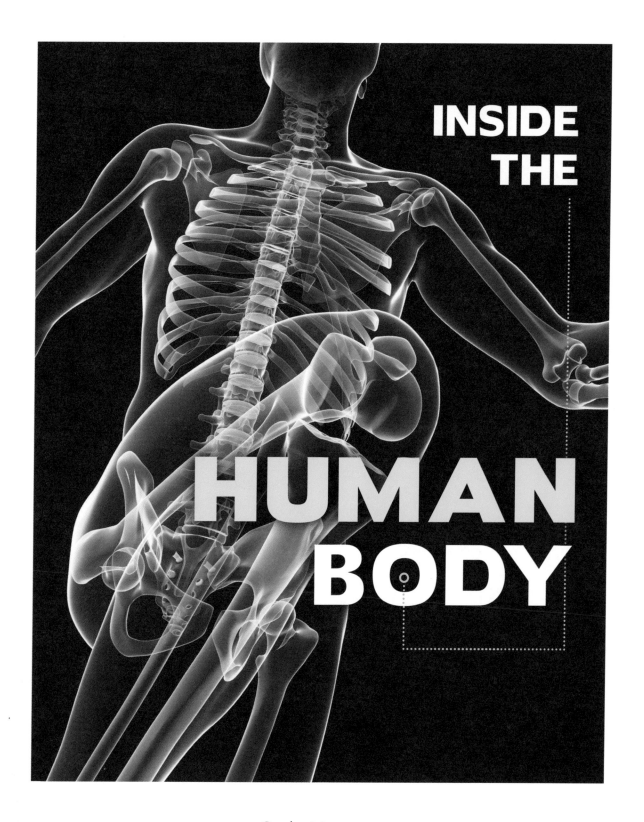

INSIDE THE HUMAN BODY

Carla Mooney

Illustrated by Tom Casteel

Nomad Press

A division of Nomad Communications

10 9 8 7 6 5 4 3 2 1

This book was manufactured by Versa Press, Inc., East Peoria, Illinois
June 2020, Job #J20-01723
ISBN Softcover: 978-1-61930-903-6
ISBN Hardcover: 978-1-61930-900-5

Educational Consultant, Marla Conn

Questions regarding the ordering of this book should be addressed to
Nomad Press
2456 Christian St., White River Junction, VT 05001
www.nomadpress.net

Printed in the United States.

Titles in the Inquire & Investigate
Human Beings set

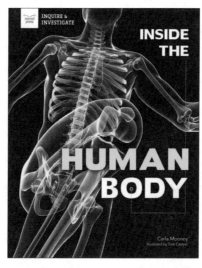

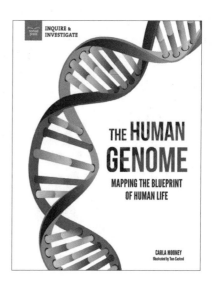

Check out more titles at www.nomadpress.net

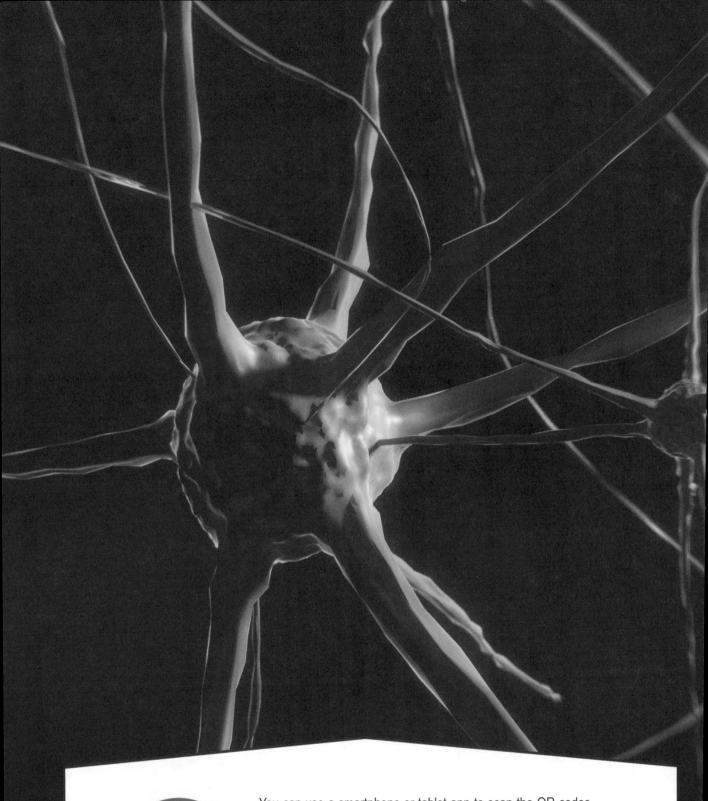

Interested in primary sources? **Look for this icon.**

You can use a smartphone or tablet app to scan the QR codes and explore more! Cover up neighboring QR codes to make sure you're scanning the right one. You can find a list of URLs on the Resources page.

If the QR code doesn't work, try searching the internet with the Keyword Prompts to find other helpful sources.

 human body

Contents

Glossary ▾ Metric Conversions ▾ Resources
Selected Bibliography ▾ Index

TIMELINE

Around 500 BCE: Ancient Greek philosopher and medical theorist Alcmaeon of Crotron makes the first recorded medical dissection of a human body.

Around 400 BCE: Greek physician Hippocrates supports the theory that the body is made of four humors or bodily fluids: black bile, phlegm, blood, and yellow bile. When the humors are out of balance, a person becomes ill.

384–322 BCE: The philosopher Aristotle distinguishes between arteries and veins. He relies on the dissection of animals instead of human bodies for his work.

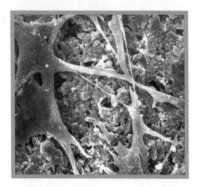

129–216 CE: Greek scientist and physician Galen moves to ancient Rome. He demonstrates that the arteries hold blood, but mistakenly believes that the blood flows back and forth from the heart in an ebb-and-flow manner. His work forms the basis of medical knowledge for centuries.

1235: The first European medical school opens at Salerno, Italy.

1490: The first anatomical theater, where students view dissections and witness human anatomy, opens in Padua, Italy.

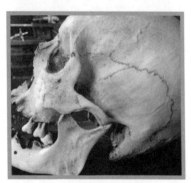

1491: The first illustrated printed medical book, *Fasciculus Medicinae* by Johannes de Ketham, is published in Venice, Italy.

1452-1519: Italian painter and inventor Leonardo da Vinci creates more than 700 detailed illustrations of the human body.

1543: Flemish physician Vesalius prints his seven-volume illustrated anatomy, *De Humani Corporis Fabrica* (*On the Workings of the Human Body*), which features detailed and accurate drawings of the dissected human body.

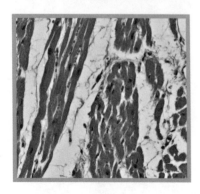

1628: English physician William Harvey correctly describes in detail the circulation and properties of blood through body and heart.

1664: Thomas Willis gives the first complete description of the anatomy of the brain.

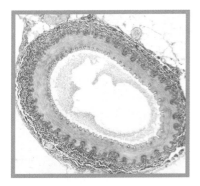

1774: English obstetrician William Hunter publishes a detailed work on the reproductive system.

1832: England passes the Anatomy Act to provide a legitimate supply of bodies and prevent body-snatching, grave-robbing, and murdering as a means of providing human bodies for dissection and study.

1839: Matthias Schleiden and Theodor Schwann introduce cell theory, the idea that the body is made up of tiny individual cells and that the cell is the basic unit of all life.

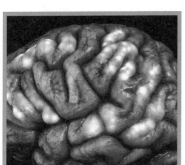

1858: English physician Henry Gray first publishes *Gray's Anatomy, Descriptive and Surgical*, a textbook of human anatomy. The latest version is still widely used today.

1895: German physicist Wilhelm Roentgen discovers X-rays, which become important in medical diagnosis and therapy.

1910: August Krogh wins the Nobel Prize for discovering how the capillaries regulate blood flow.

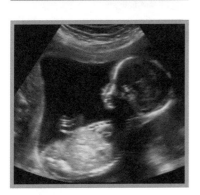

1952: Felix Bloch and Edward Purcell receive the Nobel Prize in physics for their work on magnetic resonance, which leads to the development of magnetic resonance imaging (MRI), a way to scan and look inside the body.

1953: James Watson and Francis Crick discover the molecular structure of DNA.

1977: Raymond Damadian builds the first magnetic resonance (MRI) body scanner and performs a full body scan.

1990: Scientists develop functional magnetic resonance imaging (fMRI) to study the brain as it works.

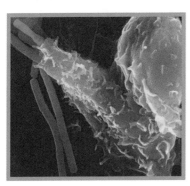

2003: The Human Genome Project completes mapping the entire sequence of DNA in human chromosomes.

2018: Doctors begin to have success treating cancer with immunotherapy, which supports the body's immune system in defeating cancer cells.

Introduction ▶

Let's Talk About the Human Body

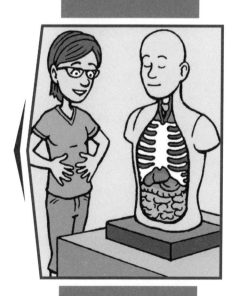

Why is it important to study anatomy?

The more we know about how our bodies work, the better able we are to stay healthy for our entire lives! Plus, the science of anatomy is fascinating.

Your body is an amazing machine! Trillions of unique cells work together to form the tissues, organs, and body systems that allow you to run and jump, laugh and cry, feel pain and joy. Some of the body's most complex workings hum along without you even realizing all the action that goes on behind the scenes.

For example, when you eat, the body's digestive system breaks down food to release essential nutrients to fuel the body. The heart and cardiovascular system pump nutrients via blood to every part of the body through a network of blood vessels. At the same time, the body's immune system stands guard, ready to jump into action to protect the body from disease and infection.

These are just a few of the amazing things the body does to sustain life.

For thousands of years, people have been curious about how the human body works. The ancient Egyptians were interested in the human body and had some knowledge about its structure, even if they didn't fully understand how it worked. Written around the seventeenth century BCE, the Edwin Smith papyrus is an ancient Egyptian medical text. The papyrus is believed to be the world's earliest known medical document. It describes different illnesses and how to treat them. But how did the ancient Egyptians learn about the human body without today's technology?

Historically, scientists who wanted to learn about the human body and its structure had to dissect bodies. Of course, it was possible to do this only after a person had died! Scientists had no way to see the body's inner workings in action.

Today, different technologies allow scientists to see inside a living body. X-rays, magnetic resonance imaging (MRI), and electron microscopes allow people to study a living human body. Using these technologies, scientists can examine the smallest parts of the body and learn how everything works together.

The Edwin Smith papyrus

Scientists who study the human body believe that every structure and process, no matter how small, is essential to the body's inner workings. Every structure and process plays its part in keeping the body alive and running like a fine-tuned machine.

> The human body is more than a structure. It is a living, working machine.

||||||||||||||||||||||||||||||||

PRIMARY SOURCES

ANATOMY VS. PHYSIOLOGY

The study of the human body is divided into two main areas—anatomy and physiology.

Anatomy is the study of how the body is structured. The human body is a complicated puzzle with bones, muscles, organs, nerves, and vessels organized in specific patterns. Anatomy can be divided into several sub-specialties.

- Gross anatomy studies the large parts of the body—the structures that the naked eye can see, including bones, muscles, the heart, lungs, and more.

- Histologic anatomy studies the different types of tissue throughout the body and the cells that make up these tissues.

- Developmental anatomy studies the life cycle of the human body and how body parts change during a person's lifespan.

- Comparative anatomy studies the similarities and differences in the structures of different species. This information can give scientists new insights into the different structures of the human body and how they function.

Physiology is the study of how the body functions. Specifically, it is the study of how cells, tissues, and organisms work. Physiologists try to answer key questions that range from the function of single cells to how the body adapts to changes in temperature and environment.

Physiology also helps scientists better understand human disease and develop new methods for treating those diseases.

IT'S ALL IN THE PERSPECTIVE

As we talk about the body in this book, it's important to have the right perspective. For example, where is left on the body? A term such as "left" can be confusing if you don't know the perspective. Is it left from the body's perspective or is it left from the viewer's perspective? Knowing the difference is pretty important, especially if a doctor is about to perform a surgery on a patient's left arm!

To be precise when describing direction and position on the human body, scientists use specific terms for position, such as anterior (front) and posterior (back). They also divide the body into planes, regions, and cavities. All of these terms tell scientists which way to look at the human body. They give scientists the proper perspective.

credit: Blausen.com staff (2014). "Medical gallery of Blausen Medical 2014." *WikiJournal of Medicine* 1 (2)

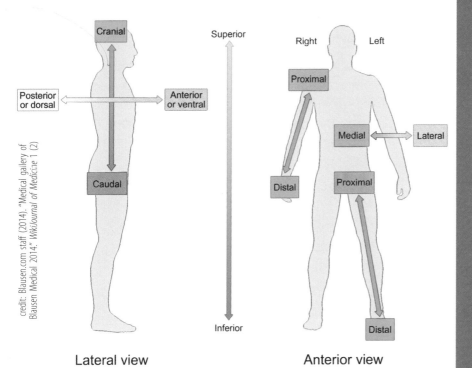

Lateral view

Anterior view

SCIENTIFIC METHOD

The scientific method is the process scientists use to ask questions and find answers. Keep a science journal to record your methods and observations during all the activities in this book. You can use a scientific method worksheet to keep your ideas and observations organized.

Question: What are we trying to find out? What problem are we trying to solve?

Research: What is already known about this topic?

Hypothesis: What do we think the answer will be?

Equipment: What supplies are we using?

Method: What procedure are we following?

Results: What happened and why?

BODY WISE

By understanding how the body works, scientists are better able to fix it when something goes wrong.

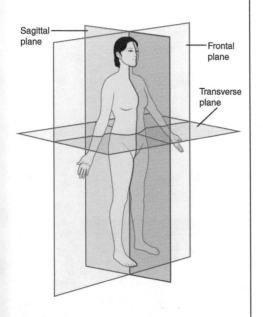

Sagittal plane

Frontal plane

Transverse plane

Here are some common anatomical terms used to describe position on the human body.

- Right: toward the body's right
- Left: toward the body's left
- Anterior/ventral: front
- Posterior/dorsal: back
- Medial: toward the middle of the body
- Lateral: on the side
- Proximal: near the point of attachment or the body's trunk
- Distal: farther from the point of attachment or the body's trunk
- Superficial: near the surface of the body
- Deep: farther from the body's surface
- Superior: higher or above another body part
- Inferior: below or lower than another body part

The body can also be divided into planes. A plane is a two-dimensional, flat surface with no thickness. Imagine sliding a flat piece of paper through a round ball. It divides the ball into two sections. Similarly, the human body and its organs can be divided into anatomical planes so that scientists know which portion of the body or organ is being discussed. Anatomical planes can pass through the body at any angle. Here are some of the more common ones.

- Frontal plane: divides the body or organ into anterior (front) and posterior (back).
- Sagittal plane: divides the body or organ lengthwise into right and left sides.
- Transverse plane: divides the body or organ horizontally into superior (top) and inferior (bottom) sections.

In anatomy, a region is a specific area on the body. First, the human body is divided into two main regions—the axial and appendicular regions. The axial body consists of everything down the center axis of the body, including the head, neck, chest, back, abdomen, and pelvis. The appendicular body includes all of the body's appendages—also known as legs and arms.

The axial body can be divided further into subregions. These include the head and neck, thorax, and abdomen. Each subregion can be divided into even smaller regions. For example, the head and neck region includes the cephalic (head), cervical (neck), cranial (skull), frontal (forehead), nasal (nose), occipital (base of skull), oral (mouth), and orbital (eyes) regions.

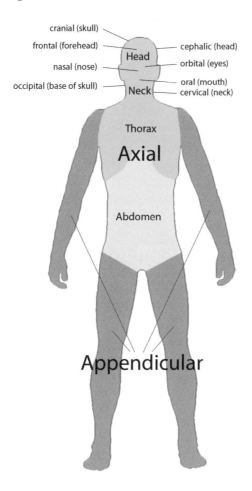

cranial (skull)
frontal (forehead)
nasal (nose)
occipital (base of skull)

cephalic (head)
orbital (eyes)
oral (mouth)
cervical (neck)

Head
Neck
Thorax
Axial
Abdomen

Appendicular

BODY CAVITIES

Body cavities are another way to identify a location on the human body. A body cavity is a space where internal organs are held. The body has two main cavities—the dorsal cavity and the ventral cavity.

The dorsal cavity is found on the posterior (back) of the body. It includes two smaller cavities—the cranial cavity, which holds the brain, and the spinal cavity, which is the space in the vertebrae that holds the spinal cord.

The ventral cavity is located on the anterior (front) of the body. It is larger than the dorsal cavity and holds many organs. The ventral cavity is divided into smaller cavities called the thoracic cavity and the abdominopelvic cavity. The thoracic cavity, which holds the heart and lungs, is further divided into the pleural cavity (lungs) and pericardial cavity (heart). The abdominopelvic cavity is divided into the abdominal cavity (stomach, intestines, spleen, liver, and other organs) and the pelvic cavity (bladder, some reproductive organs, and rectum).

Watch this video for more information on different anatomical terms!

 anatomy position video

BODY WISE

The human body is 55 to 60 percent water. Your brain is about 80 percent water.

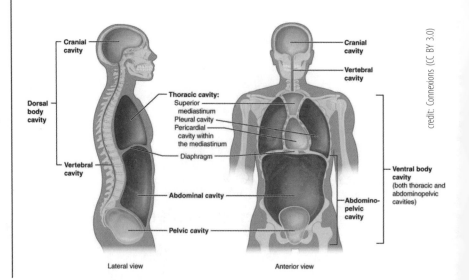

credit: Connexions (CC BY 3.0)

LEVELS OF ORGANIZATION

The human body is organized into several physical levels, which scientists call levels of organization. These levels are the cellular level, the tissue level, the organ level, the organ system level, and the organism level.

Imagine you are building a human body. You would need building blocks at the smallest level—the cellular level—to create tissues. Tissues combine to form organs. Organs work together with other organs to form organ systems. Finally, all of the body's organ systems interact and work together to form a complete organism—your human body! Let's take a closer look at this structure.

> All living things are made of cells. These tiny building blocks of life can be seen with a powerful microscope.

Inside the cells, almost all of the body's functions take place, from transforming energy to producing proteins. Millions of cells join and work together to create tissue.

Tissue is a structure made of cells that has a specific function. Connective tissue supports body parts and holds them together. Muscle tissue allows your body to move. Nervous tissue forms nerves and sends impulses throughout the body. Epithelial tissues line and cover organs and are involved in the absorption and secretion of substances.

Groups of tissues combine to form organs. An organ performs a specific function. For example, the heart is an organ that pumps blood throughout the body. Organs are made of at least two different tissue types, and many contain several types of tissue.

BACK TO ROOTS

When talking about the human body, there are certain words or word fragments that scientists frequently use. Take a look!

Word Root	Meaning	Body System
os-, oste- arth-	bone or joint	skeletal system
myo-, sarco-	muscle	muscular system
neur-	nerve	nervous system
card-, angi- hema, vaso-	heart, vessel, blood vessels	cardiovascular system
pulmon-, bronch-	lung, windpipe	respiratory system
gastr-, enter-, dent-, hepat-	stomach intestine, teeth, liver	digestive system
aden-, estr-	endocrine system	gland, steroid
ren-, neph-, ur-	kidney, urinary	urinary system
lymph-, leuk-, itis	lymph, white, inflammation	lymphatic system

Groups of organs work together in organ systems to meet a specific need. For example, the respiratory system is responsible for two very important functions. It brings a constant supply of oxygen into the body, which is necessary for cells to survive. It also removes carbon dioxide, which is a waste product of cellular functions. The organs of the respiratory system—the nose, pharynx, larynx, trachea, bronchi, and lungs—work together to perform these functions.

All organ systems work together to support an organism.

IIIIIIIIIIIIIIIIIIIIIIIIIIIIIIIII

In this book, we'll peel back the layers of your body to take a look inside this amazing machine and learn the basic anatomy of the human body.

We'll also explore the body's physiology and how its organs work together to allow us to function and survive. Take a ride through the different organ systems and investigate the role of each in operating our human body machine.

We'll examine some of the diseases that can affect the human body and learn what we can do to keep healthy and fit. As we learn more about the human body, science is finding new ways to treat and cure all types of disease and conditions, helping people live life to the fullest.

VOCAB LAB

Write down what you think each word means. What root words can you find to help you? What does the context of the word tell you?

anatomy, **anterior**, **cell**, **inferior**, **lateral**, **medial**, **nutrients**, **organ**, **organ system**, **physiology**, **superior**, and **tissue**.

Compare your definitions with those of your friends or classmates. Did you all come up with the same meanings? Turn to the text and glossary if you need help.

KEY QUESTIONS

- **Why is the study of the human body important?**
- **What is the difference between anatomy and physiology?**
- **What are the body's levels of organization?**

Chapter 1 ▶
Start With the Cells

Why are cells considered the building blocks of the body?

Life starts with cells! Inside every cell are smaller parts that do the work necessary for your body to move, breath, and function.

To understand the human body, let's start by looking at the basic building block of life— the cell. All organisms, including humans, are made up of cells. Some organisms have only one cell, but a lot of organisms are a combination of many cells. Each cell is a complex unit that combines with other cells to form body tissues, organs, and organ systems.

The human body is made up of trillions of cells that make life possible. So, what do cells do?

Cells provide structure to the human body, take nutrients from food, convert those nutrients into food, and carry out other essential functions. Cells also hold the body's instruction manual in the form of genetic material. In our bodies, cells vary widely from simple skin cells to highly specialized nerve cells.

Humans have many types of cells. Each type of cell has a different purpose. Let's shrink down and take a closer look!

INSIDE THE CELL

Although the human body has many different types of cells, all cells have many of the same components. Each component plays a role in keeping the cell healthy and working as intended.

A cell membrane surrounds each cell. Like a plastic bag, the membrane holds all the cell's parts and fluids inside the cell, while keeping anything that doesn't belong in the cell on the outside.

Inside the cell membrane, a jelly-like fluid called cytoplasm fills the cell. Within the cytoplasm, a cytoskeleton supports the cell and gives it structure. The cytoskeleton also makes it possible for substances to move within a cell. Also found in the cytoplasm are specialized structures called organelles. Each organelle has its own specific job to perform.

The largest organelle in the cell—the nucleus—is the brain of the cell. The nucleus tells the cell when to grow, mature, divide, and die. It carries one complete copy of the organism's DNA (deoxyribonucleic acid), the cell's unique genetic material. DNA is the cell's instruction manual.

Using genes located on the DNA, the nucleus tells the organelles what to do. A membrane called the nuclear envelope surrounds the nucleus, protecting its DNA and separating it from the rest of the cell.

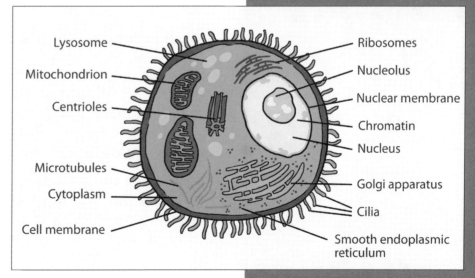

Lysosome
Mitochondrion
Centrioles
Microtubules
Cytoplasm
Cell membrane
Ribosomes
Nucleolus
Nuclear membrane
Chromatin
Nucleus
Golgi apparatus
Cilia
Smooth endoplasmic reticulum

There are many other organelles in the cell. Here are a few, along with what they do.

- **Mitochondria:** These organelles are the cell's energy factories. They convert nutrients from food into energy in the form of adenosine triphosphate (ATP) that the cell can use. ATP is a kind of energy that fuels many of the cell's activities. Cells that need a lot of energy, such as muscle cells, can have several thousand mitochondria.

- **Ribosomes:** These organelles are the cell's protein makers. Ribosomes receive information from the cell's genetic instructions and use it to build proteins by connecting amino acids. Ribosomes either float freely in the cytoplasm or are connected to the endoplasmic reticulum.

- **Endoplasmic reticulum (ER):** This network of tubules processes molecules created by the cell and transports them to specific places inside or outside the cell. The ER works closely with the Golgi apparatus and ribosomes. Rough ER is covered with ribosomes and produces proteins. Smooth ER contains enzymes that create lipids (fats).

- **Golgi apparatus:** This is a packaging organelle in the cell. The Golgi apparatus gathers simple molecules and combines them to make more complex molecules. Then, it takes those bigger molecules and packages them into what's called vesicles, which are either stored for later use or sent out of the cell.

- **Lysosomes and peroxisomes:** These organelles hold digestive enzymes made by the cell. They digest food particles and worn-out parts of the cell and break down toxic materials in the cell.

BUILDING MORE CELLS

The cells in the human body perform several functions that are essential to life. One of their most important jobs is creating new cells.

Organisms begin life as a single cell. While some organisms remain single-celled, others grow to have many cells. For this to happen, one cell divides into two cells. Two cells divide into four, four cells divide into eight, and so on. Each new cell is a complete copy of the original cell. Through this cell division—a process called mitosis—an organism builds itself from a single cell.

Every cell has a life cycle, called the cell cycle. The cell cycle has four stages. First, the cell increases in size. Second, the cell copies its DNA. Third, the cell prepares to divide. Finally, the cell divides in mitosis.

Once cell division is complete, each new cell may begin to differentiate. Not every cell in the body has the same job. Muscle cells are different from brain cells. And blood cells are different from skin cells.

Think about what happens when kids graduate from high school. Not all kids do the same thing. Some may start work immediately. Others may join the military or go to college. Each one is on a path of differentiation that prepares them for different jobs in the community—maybe as police officers, plumbers, soldiers, teachers, doctors, salespeople, or engineers. In a similar way, the process of differentiation in cells enables them to develop the structures and functions that they will need for their jobs in the body. The structure and function of a cell are determined by the type of proteins present in it.

Mitosis in action

WHAT ARE AMINO ACIDS?

Amino acids are molecules used by cells to make proteins. The human body has 20 different kinds of amino acids. The main elements in amino acids are carbon, oxygen, nitrogen, and hydrogen. The human body makes some amino acids and gets others from food. To make a protein, the cell's ribosomes string together long chains of amino acids. The sequence of the amino acids determines the type of protein that is created. The human body has thousands of different proteins. Proteins help determine the traits of an organism and trigger cellular processes. Each has a function to help the human body survive.

MAKING PROTEINS

A major function of cells is to build proteins and other products. Proteins are incredibly important in your body! The body uses proteins as building materials, to make enzymes that regulate chemical reactions, and to produce hormones and other important substances. The type and function of a cell depends on the kinds of proteins it makes.

A cell makes proteins in a process called protein synthesis. Protein synthesis begins in the cell's nucleus. Certain genes in the DNA become active and trigger the production of a specific protein molecule. The nucleus uses RNA—ribonucleic acid—to send instructions about how to build the protein to the ribosomes.

The ribosomes work closely with the ER and Golgi apparatus to package and transport the proteins once they are complete.

PASSIVE TRANSPORT

You might think cells are quiet, still places, but, in fact, they're very active. There's a lot going on and many different kinds of give and take.

Cells interact with the fluids around them by exchanging substances. The cell's survival depends on its ability to maintain the right balance between material inside and outside the cell.

This movement of substances between cells and body fluids can occur in several ways, including passive transport and active transport. Passive transport happens naturally and doesn't require energy to accomplish.

A cell membrane is semi-permeable. This means it allows some materials, such as small molecules, to move in and out of the cell. The substances flow from one side of the membrane to the other naturally. One method of passive transport is diffusion, which happens when substances move from an area of higher concentration to an area of lower concentration.

Sometimes, there is a large difference in the concentration of a particular molecule inside and outside the cell. For example, a cell might be surrounded by a very high oxygen molecule concentration, but have a low oxygen concentration inside the cell. If this is the case, the oxygen molecules outside the cell are small enough to move through the cell membrane and enter the cell.

Diffusion uses no energy. It continues until the concentration of oxygen molecules inside and outside the cell is in balance, or reaches equilibrium.

Osmosis is another example of passive transport—this process involves water molecules. Just as with diffusion, a concentration difference causes the movement of water across the cell membrane until both sides are equal.

Filtration is another passive mode of transport. In filtration, pressure on a solution on one side of the cell membrane forces the fluid through the membrane. The more pressure, the faster the substances will pass through. You might see an example of filtration happen in your own home when you turn on a faucet. The water pressure is released and pushes water out of the tap.

Every organelle has an important role in the cell and therefore in the body as a whole. Check out the functions of some of the organelles and the roles of different kinds of cells in this animated video!

Cell Structure
Nucleus
Medical Media

BODY WISE

Cells make many different products. Some cells make and transport a single product, while other cells make several products and perform other functions.

POWERING THE CELL

Cells—just like people—need energy to function. This energy takes the form of ATP, which is a chemical fuel used to power the processes of a cell. Inside the cell, mitochondria transform energy from nutrients into ATP. ATP is made from a string of nitrogen-containing compounds (adenine) connected to a five-carbon sugar (ribose) to form adenosine. The adenosine bonds to three phosphate (or triphosphate) groups. The chemical bonds between the phosphate groups hold energy. When those bonds are broken, energy is released for the cell to use!

ACTIVE TRANSPORT

Passive transport works well for smaller molecules, but what about big ones? To transport larger molecules through the cell membrane, the cell uses a process called active transport. Unlike passive transport, active transport requires energy.

The energy for active transport comes from ATP. Remember, ATP is energy that is formed in a cell's mitochondria. Proteins in the cell's membrane do much of the work in active transport. Each protein has a specific job. One that moves a glucose molecule will not move a calcium molecule.

Large molecules need to be packaged into what's called a vesicle. The vesicle's outer membrane is made of the same material as the cell membrane. When moving the molecule out of the cell in a process called exocytosis, the molecules in the vesicle's membrane fuse with the molecules of the cell membrane. This causes the vesicle to push its contents out of the cell. The reverse process, called endocytosis, brings a large molecule into the cell.

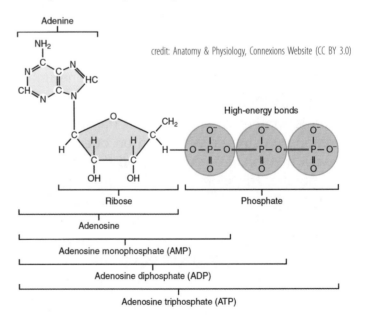

credit: Anatomy & Physiology, Connexions Website (CC BY 3.0)

CELLS FORM TISSUES

In the human body, groups of cells form tissue. Not all the cells in a tissue are the same, but they all work together to carry out a specific function. The human body has four main categories of tissue.

- Connective tissue connects, supports, and binds body structures together. It includes bone, cartilage, and adipose tissue. In some parts of the body, connective tissue such as bone supports the weight of other structures.

- Epithelial tissue is used for coverings and linings in the body. This type of tissue forms the epidermis of the skin and its structures, covers the body's internal organs, and forms the lining of blood vessels and some organs.

- Muscle tissues are central to movement and other important body functions.

- Nervous tissue can be found in the brain, spinal cord, and nerves. It coordinates and controls many of the body's activities. Nervous tissue sends messages to contract muscles, gathers information about the environment, and is involved in emotions, memory, and reasoning.

Now that you know something about the building blocks within our bodies, let's look at some of the body systems that cells make up. Let's start with the musculoskeletal system, because without that, you wouldn't even be upright!

VOCAB LAB

Write down what you think each word means. What root words can you find to help you? What does the context of the word tell you?

adenosine triphosphate, **connective tissue**, **cytoplasm**, **membrane**, **mitochondria**, **mitosis**, **nucleus**, **organelle**, and **ribosome**.

Compare your definitions with those of your friends or classmates. Did you all come up with the same meanings? Turn to the text and glossary if you need help.

TEXT TO WORLD

How are your cells similar to your body as a whole?

KEY QUESTIONS

- **What are two ways that material enters and exits the cell?**

- **Why do cells differentiate?**

- **What essential functions does a cell perform?**

Ideas for Supplies ▼

- 4 raw eggs
- white vinegar
- 4 different types of liquids, such as tap water, salt water, corn syrup, and more.
- 4 clear glasses that can hold 1 cup of liquid and an egg

To investigate more, consider what happens if you dissolve a substance such as sugar, ground coffee, cocoa, or iced tea powder in water and then submerge the egg in it. Does this change how the egg reacts to the water? Explain your observations.

EGG EXPERIMENT

We've seen how cells have semi-permeable membranes that allow certain molecules to enter and exit the cells. Diffusion occurs when molecules move from an area of higher concentration to an area of lower concentration. This movement continues until equilibrium is reached—the concentration of the molecule on both sides of the membrane is equal.

You can replicate how the membrane for a human cell blocks certain substances and lets others enter. Using white vinegar, you can harden a raw egg and dissolve its shell so that it will act like a cell with a semi-permeable membrane. How will the egg react to different substances?

- **Carefully place the eggs in a bowl and cover with white vinegar.** Soak the eggs for three days. Each day, take notes in your science journal on how the eggs look and feel.

- **On day four, take the eggs out of the bowl and rinse them with water.** How do they feel? What happened to the shells? Measure each egg's length and width.

- **Pour 1 cup of the four liquids into four separate glasses.** Let the eggs sit in the liquids for four more days. Each day, measure the eggs and write down your observations.

- **After the four days, take the eggs that were not placed in tap water, rinse them, and put them into separate glasses of water for four additional days.** Record your observations. What effects did each liquid have on the eggs? How did your observations relate to cell diffusion?

Chapter 2 ▶
Move It with Muscles and Bones

Why do we need both bones and muscles in order to move?

While bones give our bodies stability and structure, muscles make it possible for us to bend, twist, leap, and everything else!

Imagine trying to ride a bike without moving your legs. How could you swing a tennis racquet with an arm that wiggled like a rope? To move your body, you need bones, joints, and muscles. Bones keep your arm straight and not floppy when you swing a tennis racquet. Joints allow you to bend your legs when you pedal a bike. And muscles make all movement possible.

The musculoskeletal system is a combination of two body systems: the skeletal system and the muscular system. The two systems work closely together to allow you to move your body. Different tissues attach the muscles, bones, and joints to each other. Ligaments connect bones to each other at joints, while tendons connect muscles to bones.

Without the musculoskeletal system, you couldn't text with your thumbs, walk to the park, play baseball, or even plop down on the couch when you're tired!

BONES: THE BODY'S FRAME

The 206 bones in the human skeleton form the basic frame for our bodies. Bones begin to develop before birth and continue to grow though adulthood. When bones first form, they are made of cartilage, a firm tissue that is softer and more flexible than bone. Newborn infants are very flexible because many of their bones are still made of cartilage. That's why when you hold a newborn, you have to support its head—newborns' heads are too heavy for their necks to hold up since their neck is made of cartilage.

Within a few weeks of birth, the bones begin the process of ossification, or the formation of new bone. During ossification, hard deposits of calcium phosphate and collagen—the two main components of bone—replace the cartilage. Ossification continues through childhood into early adulthood.

Do you track your height to see how much taller you're getting? Your doctor probably does when you go for a checkup. You get taller because your bones are still getting longer. This stops around age 18 in females and 21 in males—at that point, your bones will not grow any longer and you will not get any taller.

Although they stop getting longer, throughout your lifetime, your bones are constantly remodeled. During remodeling, old bone is broken down and digested by the body and new bone is formed.

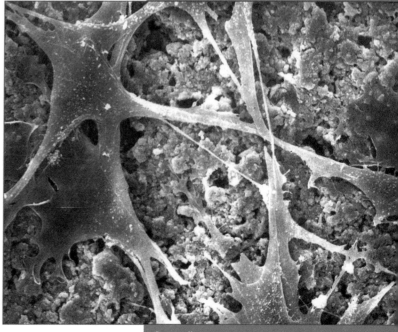

Bone cells
credit: H.Xu/American Dental Association Foundation

Bone growth and remodeling depend on specialized cells called osteocytes. There are two types of osteocytes—osteoblasts and osteoclasts. Osteoblasts form new bone and are often found on the surface of new bone. Osteoclasts are large cells that dissolve and resorb old or damaged bone tissue. Together, these cells help keep bone healthy!

TYPES OF BONES

Not all bones are the same. The bones in the body can be grouped into five categories by shape—short, flat, long, sesamoid, and irregular.

Short bones are small, solid, and often shaped like cubes. The carpals in your wrists are short bones that connect your hands to your arms. The tarsals in your ankles connect your feet to your legs. They allow for some movement.

Flat bones are generally flat or slightly curved. They might vary in thickness. Flat bones protect the body's organs like shields. The ribs and sternum in the chest are flat bones that protect the heart. The ilium bone, which forms the upper part of the pelvis, the clavicle (collar bone), and scapula (shoulder blade) are all flat bones. The skull, which protects the brain, is made up of flat bones.

In addition to protecting organs, flat bones provide large areas for muscles to attach. Many of these bones form the axial skeleton, the central part of the skeleton.

Learn more about the different bones in your body in this video!

(PS)

3D4Medical skeletal

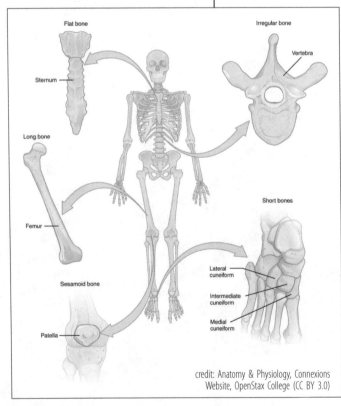

credit: Anatomy & Physiology, Connexions Website, OpenStax College (CC BY 3.0)

Long bones provide the main support for the appendicular skeleton, which includes your legs and arms. These long bones are attached to the axial skeleton. Long bones have a long shaft with two ends.

> The longest bone in the body, the femur in the leg, is a long bone.

Many long bones support the body's weight and help it move. Other long bones include the rest of the leg bones (fibula and tibia) and arm bones (radius, ulna, humerus).

Sesamoid bones are small, round bones embedded in tendons. Sesamoid bones protect tendons from stress and wear. The kneecap, or patella, is the largest sesamoid bone in your body.

Some bones don't fit into any category. These irregular bones vary in shape, size, and structure. The vertebrae that protect the spinal cord are an example of irregular bones. They form a tunnel around the spinal cord. The vertebrae have several protrusions where muscles, tendons, and ligaments attach to them. Other irregular bones include the coccyx and sacrum in the tailbone and the ischium and pubis in the pelvis.

WHAT ARE BONES MADE OF?

Have you ever heard the saying that something is as strong as bone? Bones are some of the strongest, hardest structures in your body. Several minerals, including calcium, phosphorus, and sodium, make bones hard and strong. Calcium makes up about 60 to 70 percent of a bone's weight.

Despite their size, small finger bones are also long bones!

IIIIIIIIIIIIIIIIIIIIIIIIIIIIIII

HELP FOR STRONG BONES

The bones in the human body experience two main types of stress: the force of gravity pulling down on them and the force of tension from muscles as they move the bones. This stress increases when you walk, run, dance, play tennis, or participate in any weight-bearing exercise. When performed regularly, this type of exercise makes bones stronger. But if you're not active and spend a lot of time sitting on the couch, you're not helping your bones!

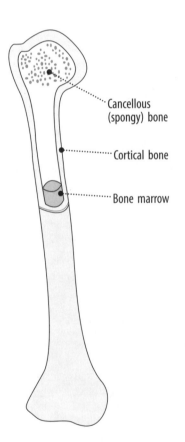

Cancellous (spongy) bone

Cortical bone

Bone marrow

The amount of calcium in a bone determines the bone's stiffness and its strength. Bones also contain a protein called collagen. Collagen gives bone its flexibility and ability to resist the pulling force of tension. Watch a gymnast bound across the gym during a floor routine—that's some pretty flexible bone! Even people who aren't professional athletes need to be able to bend, twist, and not snap in half if they fall. That's why collagen is an important part of bone.

A bone is made of two types of tissue—cortical bone and cancellous bone. Cortical bone is very dense. Cortical bone can survive heavy loads and the force of muscle tension before it fails and breaks. About 80 percent of the human skeleton is cortical bone. Although it looks solid, cortical bone actually has many passageways for blood vessels and nerves.

Inside cortical bone, you'll find cancellous bone, a spongy tissue that is less dense than cortical bone, making it more flexible. Cancellous bone can absorb energy and distribute loads that are applied to the skeleton.

JOINTS CONNECT THE BONES

If all your bones were joined together, you would have trouble moving! Luckily, your skeleton has joints, the places where two bones meet. Without joints, you would not be able to bend your arm or type with your fingers. Joints allow you to curl your toes and lift your legs.

Not all joints move the same way or have the same range of motion. Some joints move freely, while others move just a little bit, and some do not move at all.

Some joints open and close like a hinge, while others allow more complex movement. Notice how your shoulder or hip joints allow movement backward, forward, and sideways.

Some joints are fixed and do not move. In adults, the joints between the skull bones are examples of immovable joints. An adult's skull is made of bony plates that protect the brain. A thin layer of fibrous connective tissue called a suture joins these plates together very tightly so they do not move. Many joints in your face are also fixed.

Other joints move slightly. These joints are connected by cartilage or slightly flexible ligaments. The disks between the vertebrae in your spine are an example of this type of joint.

Each vertebra in the spine moves a little in relation to the bones above and below it. Together, these small movements give the spine its flexibility.

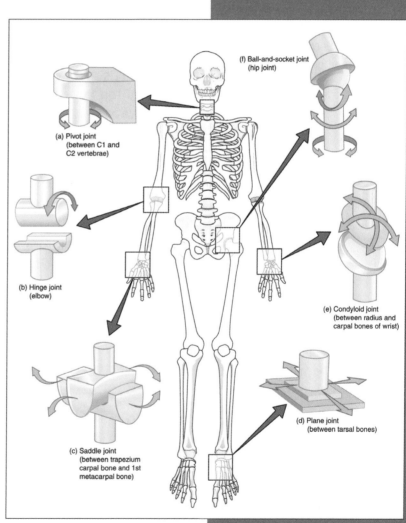

(a) Pivot joint (between C1 and C2 vertebrae)

(b) Hinge joint (elbow)

(c) Saddle joint (between trapezium carpal bone and 1st metacarpal bone)

(d) Plane joint (between tarsal bones)

(e) Condyloid joint (between radius and carpal bones of wrist)

(f) Ball-and-socket joint (hip joint)

credit: Anatomy & Physiology, Connexions Website, OpenStax College (CC BY 3.0)

WATERY BONES

Bones contain water, which delivers nutrients and removes wastes from bone tissue. A healthy bone has about 25 to 30 percent of its weight in water. If a bone's water content decreases, it becomes more brittle and breaks more easily.

Check out this video about the muscular system and how it works! What do the root words "myo" and "sarco" mean?

 Crash Course muscular system

Most joints in the body can move in many directions. These joints, sometimes called synovial joints, form where two bones are joined together by ligaments. Cartilage cushions the end of each bone, and a membrane-lined cavity filled with synovial fluid lubricates and cushions the joint. Joints at your elbows, shoulders, and ankles are examples of moveable joints.

There are three main types of moveable joints.

- Hinge joints allow movement in one direction. The joints at your knees and elbows are examples of hinge joints. You can bend and straighten your knee, but you cannot move it sideways.

- Pivot joints allow a rotating or twisting motion. A pivot joint at the top of the vertebral column allows you to move your head from side to side.

- In a ball-and-socket joint, the round end of a long bone fits into a depression called a socket in another bone. This type of joint can move in many directions and can rotate. Joints at your hips and shoulders are ball-and-socket joints.

CONNECTIVE TISSUE HOLDS IT TOGETHER

Although many bones fit together well, they need a little more support so that you can walk, run, and jump. That's where connective tissue plays a role. Connective tissues, which include tendons, ligaments, and joint capsules, provide the support your skeleton needs for movement.

- A tendon is a soft tissue that connects a muscle to a bone. When the tendon of a muscle crosses a joint, that joint will move when the muscle contracts. The kind of movement depends on the position, length of the tendon, and the type of joint.

- Ligaments are bands of tissue that connect two bones and hold each bone in place. Ligaments can be found around your knees, ankles, elbows, shoulders, and other joints.

- Joint capsules surround a joint and enclose the joint cavity with a membrane, which holds protective synovial fluid. When two bones that connect at a joint move, they can rub and cause friction, eventually causing pain. The synovial fluid in the joint capsule helps protect the joint and its cartilage from friction.

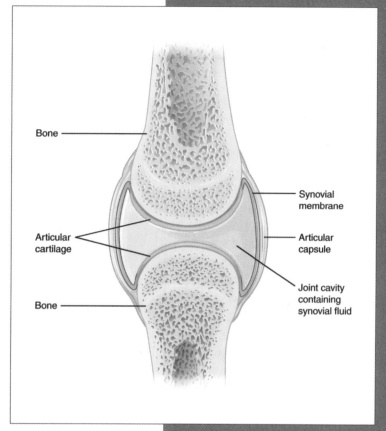

credit: Anatomy & Physiology, Connexions Website, OpenStax College (CC BY 3.0)

Along with providing support to the joints, tendons and ligaments help the body move. When a muscle contracts, it generates a force. The tendons and ligaments deliver this force to the bone, which makes it move. As the bone moves, tendons and ligaments stretch.

Typically, after stretching, tendons and ligaments return to their normal length.

You probably know someone who has broken a bone. Ouch! After a doctor sets the bone to make sure it heals properly, the human body does a pretty amazing repair job. When the bone first breaks, blood collects to form a type of scab over the broken parts. Then, a tougher tissue, called collagen, grows over the broken area. The collagen, along with cartilage, bridges the gap between the two sides of the broken bone. As time passes, this bridge hardens. Meanwhile, the healing bone needs to be protected from stress. That's why people use crutches and casts when they have a broken bone. It can take months for a bone to harden back to normal.

MUSCLES PROVIDE MOTION

While bones support your body, muscles provide the force and power needed to move. When you sit in a chair, hit a golf ball, or turn your head, muscles make it happen. Even when you are perfectly still, muscles in the body are constantly moving.

Muscles allow your heart to beat and your chest to rise and fall while you breathe. Muscles even help you communicate by moving your mouth and tongue to talk, smile, and frown.

Like every other tissue in the body, muscles are made of individual cells. Muscle cells are called fibers and are shaped like long, thin cylinders. Individual muscle fibers are bundled into fascicles. Thousands of fascicles join together to form a muscle. All of a muscle's fascicles work together to contract at the same time to produce movement.

When stimulated by a nerve impulse, a muscle contracts to produce motion. The muscle relaxes when the impulse is removed. This cycle of contraction and relaxation creates all the movement in your body. The part of the body that moves depends on where the muscle is attached.

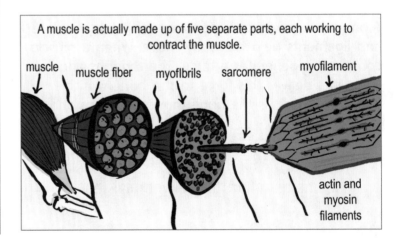

A muscle is actually made up of five separate parts, each working to contract the muscle.

muscle   muscle fiber   myoflbrils   sarcomere   myofilament

actin and myosin filaments

When a muscle attached to your arm bone is stimulated, your arm moves. Your leg won't move because it is not attached to the muscle that was stimulated.

Most skeletal muscles are attached to a bone at two or more places. The origin of a muscle is a fixed attachment that does not move. The opposite end of the muscle is called the insertion point. The insertion point is an attachment on a bone that usually moves during an action. For example, the upper arm bone, or the humerus, has a large muscle called the biceps brachii on it. The biceps muscle's origin point is at the scapula, while its insertion point is on the radius bone of the forearm. When the biceps muscle contracts, it moves the radius bone. The scapula and upper arm, or the origin, do not move.

Muscles often work in pairs. One muscle contracts and pulls a bone in one direction. However, it cannot push the muscle back in the opposite direction. Instead, the muscle relaxes and its partner muscle contracts and pulls the bone back. Think again about your arm. When you move it up and down from your elbow joint, you are using two different muscles. The biceps brachii flex your arm up and the triceps brachii extend your arm back out.

TYPES OF MUSCLES

The human body has three main types of muscles: skeletal, smooth or involuntary, and cardiac.

Skeletal muscles attach to bones in the legs, arms, abdomen, chest, neck, and face. The brachii we discussed earlier are an example of skeletal muscles. They hold the skeleton together, which gives the body its shape, and move all the different parts of the skeleton.

If they stretch too far or too often, tendons and ligaments can become loose, which affects their ability to protect and stabilize a joint. In some cases, the ligaments cannot return to their normal length and require surgery.

||||||||||||||||||||||||||||||||||||

BODY WISE

The human body has more than 600 muscles. About half a person's body weight is from muscle.

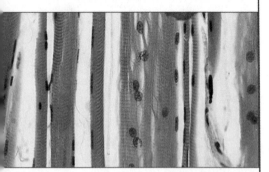

Skeletal muscle fibers

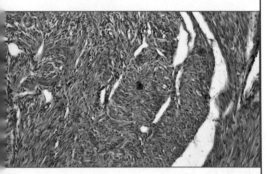

Smooth muscle tissue

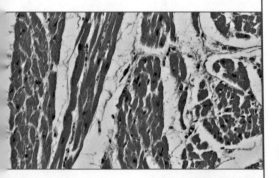

Cardiac muscle

Sometimes, they're called voluntary muscles because you can control when and how they move. Skeletal muscles are made of long cells called muscle fibers that can contract quickly and powerfully. When looked at under a microscope, the fibers that make up skeletal muscles have horizontal stripes, giving the muscle a striated appearance.

Smooth muscles, also called involuntary muscles, are automatically controlled by your nervous system. You will learn more about the nervous system in Chapter 5. You do not have to think about contracting involuntary muscles because the nervous system does it for you. For example, the smooth muscles of your stomach and intestines work to digest food without you thinking about it. In your eyes, smooth muscles let you focus on objects.

Smooth muscles take longer to contract than skeletal muscles, but can stay contracted for long periods of time because they do not tire easily. Smooth muscles are also made of fibers, but they don't appear striated. As their name suggests, they look smooth under a microscope.

Cardiac muscle is found in your heart. Like smooth muscle, cardiac muscle is involuntary. It contracts when it receives a signal to make a heartbeat. The heart's powerful contractions pump blood out of the heart. You will learn about the heart and blood in the next chapter.

KEY QUESTIONS

- **How do muscles and bones work together to produce movement?**
- **What can you do to keep your bones and muscles healthy?**
- **Why is it important for bones to be flexible?**

FLEX YOUR BONES!

What happens when bones lose their strength or flexibility? The next time you have a chicken for dinner, save the bones for your experiments.

- **Find two clean chicken bones about the same size and shape.** Put one chicken bone in a glass and cover it completely with vinegar. Cover the top of the glass with plastic wrap. Let the bone soak for three or four days.

- **Remove the bone from the vinegar and dry it.** Try to bend it. What happens? How does the bone feel? Does the bone bend easily? How does it compare to the chicken bone that wasn't soaked in vinegar.

- **Next, get two more chicken bones of about the same size and shape.** Put one of the bones on a baking sheet and bake it in the oven at 250 degrees Fahrenheit for about three hours.

- **Remove the pan from the oven and let the bone cool for at least 15 minutes.** Once it has cooled enough to touch, try to bend the bone that was baked. What happens? How does it feel?

- **Now try to bend the bone that was not baked.** What happens? How does it feel compared to the baked bone? Does it bend easily? What happens when you try to break it?

To investigate more, repeat the experiment while changing some of the variables, such as the time the bone soaks in vinegar, the type of bone used, or the time the bone is baked. How do these changes affect your results? Create a chart or other visual way to present your results.

Ideas for Supplies ▼

- poster board
- straight pin
- large paper clip
- long balloons

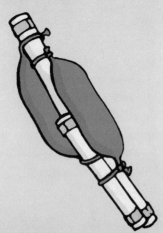

To investigate more, consider what would happen if you removed one of the muscles from the arm model. How would that affect the arm's movement?

BUILD A WORKING ARM MUSCLE

How many times a day do you use your arm? In this activity, you'll create a model of a working arm muscle to see how the muscles in your arm work together to help you bend your elbow and move your arm.

- **Do some research into arm bones and muscles.** You'll want to understand how an arm is put together.

- **Cut two 8-by-11-inch pieces and one 12-by-11-inch piece from the poster board.** Roll each piece and secure it with masking tape. What arm bones do the shorter pieces represent? What bone does the longer roll represent? Label each bone.

- **Using a long straight pin, poke a hole through the humerus, about a half-inch from its right end.** Poke holes through the radius and ulna about a half-inch from the left ends.

- **Lay the paper bones on a flat surface.** Straighten a large paper clip to create a long wire and push it through the holes to connect the bones. Bend the wire at each end to stop it from pulling out of the bone. Place tape over each wire end to prevent it from popping the balloon muscles that you will create.

- **Partially inflate two long, thin balloons and leave a tail at each end.** What arm muscles do the balloons represent? Attach the muscle balloons to the paper arms.

- **Test your arm model and observe the muscle action.** What happens to the muscles when the arm is straight and bent? When it's moving? Where else in the body does a muscle pair work like this?

Chapter 3

Pumping Life: The Cardiovascular System

What role does blood play in your body?

Both blood and the heart are vital to life! The heart sends the blood where it needs to go and the blood delivers what the body needs to stay healthy and functioning.

What's the hardest working muscle in your body? The heart! It never takes a break. It just keeps beating in your chest and sending blood throughout the body. The heart, along with the blood vessels, make up the body's cardiovascular system, pump life-giving oxygen and nutrients via the blood to the body's cells, and remove waste products. That's a big job!

About the size of a fist, the heart is a muscle that lies beneath the sternum in the thoracic cavity between the lungs. It contracts and relaxes about 70 times a minute without you even thinking about it. This keeps blood flowing through your body. Without a heart, there would be no you.

AT THE HEART OF IT

The heart is an essential part of your body, and life isn't possible if there's no heart. What does this vital organ look and behave like? Let's take a look.

The heart is made of several different parts. A protective sac called the pericardium surrounds the heart. The heart's wall is made up of an outer layer called the epicardium, a middle layer called the myocardium, and an inner layer called the endocardium. The myocardium is the thickest layer and forms most of the heart wall. Its striated muscle fibers cause the heart to contract.

The heart has four hollow chambers. The top part of the heart has the left and right atria. The bottom part has the left and right ventricles. The atria receive blood returning to the heart and send it to the ventricles. The right atrium receives blood from the body's main veins. As the right atrium contracts, blood flows into the right ventricle. When the ventricle contracts, the blood exits the heart and flows into the pulmonary artery and travels to the lungs, where it picks up oxygen. The pulmonary vein delivers oxygen-rich blood to the heart's left atrium. As the left atrium contracts, it pushes the blood into the left ventricle.

> When the left ventricle contracts, it pumps the blood out of the heart and into the body's main artery, the aorta, and to the rest of the body.

Valves between the heart's chambers allow the blood to flow forward through the heart and prevent it from flowing backward. The opening and closing of the heart's valves creates the familiar "lub-dub" sound of your heartbeat.

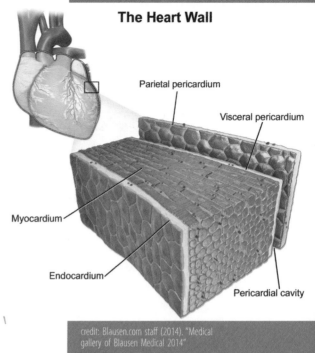

The Heart Wall

Parietal pericardium
Visceral pericardium
Myocardium
Endocardium
Pericardial cavity

credit: Blausen.com staff (2014). "Medical gallery of Blausen Medical 2014"

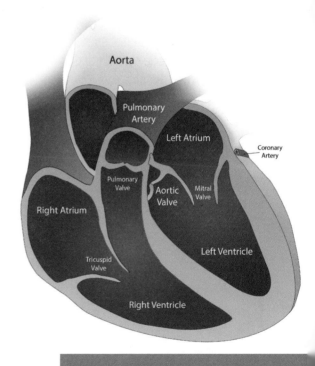

Aorta
Pulmonary Artery
Left Atrium
Coronary Artery
Pulmonary Valve
Aortic Valve
Mitral Valve
Right Atrium
Left Ventricle
Tricuspid Valve
Right Ventricle

Follow the blood through your heart!

 KidsKnowIt
beating heart

BODY WISE

How does the heart know when to contract? A special patch of muscle acts as a natural pacemaker. It generates an electrical signal between 60 and 100 times per minute that makes the heart muscle contract and relax. When the atria contract, they push blood from the atria chambers through valves into the ventricles.

THE CARDIAC CYCLE

The cardiac cycle is the period from the beginning of one heartbeat to the beginning of the next heartbeat. The cardiac cycle has two phases: systole and diastole. At the beginning of systole, the ventricles contract. This increases the blood pressure in the ventricles, which push the blood into the aorta (the body's main artery) and the pulmonary artery.

Once the ventricles are empty and relaxed, blood pressure in the ventricles falls below the pressure in the pulmonary artery and the aorta, and diastole begins as valves close to prevent the backward flow of blood into the ventricles. Blood flows from the atria and refills the ventricles. As the ventricles become full, the atria contract to push the remaining blood into the ventricles. A new cardiac cycle begins.

YOUR BLOOD: WHAT'S IN IT?

The heart works hard to keep blood moving throughout the body. What is so important about blood? And why does your body need it?

Blood is a specialized fluid made up of plasma, red blood cells, white blood cells, and platelets. Blood is about 55 percent plasma and 45 percent blood cells. Plasma is a straw-colored fluid that transports blood cells throughout the body. Plasma also carries water molecules, dissolved salts, hormones, fats, sugars, proteins, antibodies, and waste products.

Red blood cells are the most common cell in the blood, making up about 40 to 45 percent of its volume. A red blood cell looks like a disk with a flattened center on both sides.

Red blood cells are made in the bone marrow—the fatty tissue inside bone cavities—and released into the blood stream. Because they have no nucleus, red blood cells can easily change shape, which helps them fit through the different blood vessels in the body. Red blood cells contain a special protein called hemoglobin that carries oxygen from the lungs to the body and picks up carbon dioxide to return to the lungs.

Hemoglobin gives blood its red color.

White blood cells, also called leukocytes, protect the body from infection. They make up about 1 percent of blood. The most common white blood cell is the neutrophil—this is also made in bone marrow. Neutrophils only live for about a day, so the body's bone marrow constantly produces new neutrophils to protect against infection. Another type of white blood cell is the lymphocyte. Lymphocytes attack various infected cells and tumors and also make antibodies, which are proteins that fight bacteria, viruses, and other foreign materials in the body.

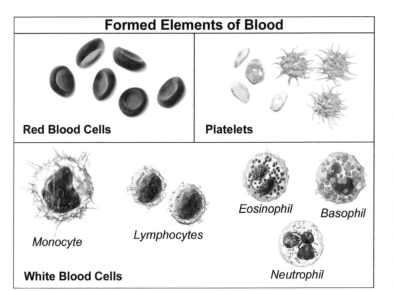

Formed Elements of Blood

Red Blood Cells

Platelets

Monocyte

Lymphocytes

Eosinophil

Basophil

Neutrophil

White Blood Cells

Platelets, also called thrombocytes, are small cell fragments. Platelets are important for blood clotting. They gather at the site of an injury and stick to the lining of the injured blood vessel. This forms a place where blood can clot. The clot covers the wound and prevents blood from leaking from the blood vessels. Have you scraped your knee recently? Platelets are what kept you from bleeding too much!

Blood has many different jobs. It transports oxygen and nutrients to the lungs and body tissues. It forms blood clots to prevent you from losing blood. It carries cells and antibodies that fight infection in the body. Blood also regulates body temperature and carries waste products to the liver and kidneys.

BLOOD'S DELIVERY SYSTEM

How do your body's cells get the oxygen and nutrients they need? They receive a delivery from your blood. Red blood cells carry oxygen molecules. A small amount of oxygen is also dissolved in plasma. When you breathe, your lungs absorb oxygen from the air. When the heart pumps blood to the lungs, red blood cells pick up that oxygen. The oxygen-carrying red blood cells return to the heart and are pumped out to the rest of the body.

As red blood cells travel throughout the body, they deliver oxygen to the body's tissues and cells.

They also pick up carbon dioxide from the cells. The blood cells return to the lungs, where the blood releases the carbon dioxide—which you breathe out—and picks up more oxygen. The entire circuit around the body takes about one minute.

All living cells in the body need important supplies to function properly. Blood carries nutrients, salts, and amino acids for building proteins. Blood also carries hormones, which are chemicals that affect the behavior of cells.

While delivering all these supplies, blood picks up waste products that cells do not need and carries them away to prevent the cells from becoming imbalanced. Blood carries waste to the kidneys, where it can be expelled from the body in urine.

Other waste is transported to the liver, where it is converted back into something the cells can use. For example, when you exercise, your muscles produce lactic acid as a byproduct. A buildup of lactic acid in muscle cells can cause a burning feeling in the muscle. Blood carries the lactic acid waste to the liver, where it is recycled back to glucose, which cells can use for energy. The glucose is then carried back to the cells by blood.

HOW BLOOD TRAVELS

How does blood get to where it needs to go in the body? The body has a complex network of blood vessels that transports blood from the top of your head to the tip of your toes and every tissue in between.

Blood travels throughout the body in five types of blood vessels: arteries, arterioles, capillaries, venules, and veins. Each vessel has a particular function in the cardiovascular system.

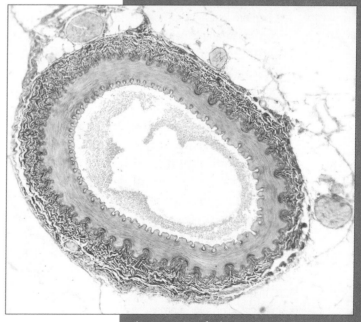

A cross section of a human artery

Capillaries are everywhere in the body, which is why you bleed anywhere that you cut your skin.

PUT THE PRESSURE ON

Your body's arteries pulse with blood in rhythm with your heartbeat. Pressure inside these blood vessels rises and falls in waves with each beat. Blood pressure is the force of blood pushing against the wall of an artery. Pressure in the arteries, called arterial pressure, is highest just after the heart contracts and lowest when the heart rests between beats. In capillaries, blood pressure is much lower. The body has so many capillaries that they spread out the force of the heart's pumping. By the time blood reaches the veins, blood pressure is low. If your arterial blood pressure is too high, it can damage the lining of the arteries. This can cause a buildup of plaque, which hardens and narrows arteries and can lead to heart disease and stroke. Some people with high blood pressure take medication to control it.

Arteries carry blood away from the heart and into the body. Because they are so close to the heart and its powerful pumping action, arteries have thick, muscular walls so they can handle high blood speeds and pressures. Their elastic walls can widen or narrow to regulate blood flow. Most arteries, except those going to the lungs, carry oxygenated blood.

As they move away from the heart, arteries divide into smaller blood vessels called arterioles. Arterioles have thinner walls than arteries. They constrict or dilate to control blood flow. From the arterioles, blood enters a network of capillaries that branch through body tissues. These very small blood vessels have thin walls that allow substances to pass through. This is when those blood cells make the exchange—oxygen, nutrients, carbon dioxide, and waste products pass to and from cells.

Capillaries connect arteries and veins. From the capillaries, blood begins its return journey to the heart. It enters the venules, which join to form veins to take blood back to the heart. This blood holds waste products collected from cells.

As they get closer to the heart, veins become larger. The superior vena cava is a large vein that delivers blood from the head and arms to the heart. The inferior vena cava transports blood from the abdomen and legs to the heart. To prevent blood from flowing backward because of gravity, the long veins in the legs have a one-way valve system that closes as blood passes through.

The heart is essential to life. Without the heart pumping blood, cells do not get the oxygen and nutrients they need to function.

TAKE CARE OF YOUR HEART

The food a person eats affects their body and its organs, including the heart. Eating a healthy diet is an important part of keeping the heart in top shape and reducing the risk of heart disease and stroke. A healthy diet includes healthy fats such as monounsaturated fats found in olive oil and avocados and omega-3 fatty acids in fish. A healthy diet also includes whole grain foods, fruits, vegetables, low-fat dairy, and protein-rich foods such as fish, eggs, and lean meats.

There are some foods to avoid when eating healthy for the heart. Eating foods with high amounts of sodium, added sugars, and saturated and trans fats can have a negative effect on the heart.

Exercise can also keep the heart healthy as it makes the heart muscle stronger. A stronger heart muscle can pump more blood each time it beats, which delivers more oxygen to the body. With more oxygen, the body is able to function more efficiently. Regular exercise can also lower a person's blood pressure and reduce their risk of heart disease.

KEY QUESTIONS

- Why are there different types of blood vessels?
- At what age is it important to care for your heart?

CPR

When a person's heart stops, cardiopulmonary resuscitation (CPR) can help save their life. CPR is an emergency procedure that involves compressing the chest to manually keep blood circulating in the body. CPR keeps the person's body and brain supplied with blood until emergency medical personnel arrive at the site. Receiving CPR as soon as the heart stops can significantly improve a person's chances of surviving cardiac arrest. Anybody can learn how to perform CPR by taking a lifesaving training class. By doing so, they may one day save a life.

TEXT TO WORLD

What kinds of heart-healthy exercise do you do?

Ideas for Supplies ▼

- butcher paper (laminated or covered with plastic if possible)
- food coloring
- various construction materials such as different sizes of rubber or vinyl tubing, straws, rubber and nitrile gloves, balloons, plastic bags, water bottles, rubber bands, a bulb pump, and more.
- funnel

CREATE A CIRCULATORY SYSTEM

The circulatory system carries essential oxygen and nutrients to every cell in the body and removes waste products, too. The entire circuit around the body takes about one minute. In this activity, you'll design your own version of the circulatory system, test it, and see where you can make improvements.

- **Use a permanent marker to trace the outline of the human body about 3 to 4 feet tall on the butcher paper.** Laminate or cover the paper with clear plastic.

- **Fill a container with water and add food coloring to make the water easier to see in the circulatory system.**

- **Research the human circulatory system and its parts.** Where does blood flow? How does it get there?

- **Using your construction materials, design and build a pump device that will move the colored water through the circulatory system.** Then create a circulatory system that will carry "blood" throughout the body. As you work, make sure your design does these things.

  - Includes a pumping device that can move fluid throughout the body

  - Has fluid that travels through the lungs

  - Has fluid that flows through most of the body

  - Prevents most of the fluid from leaking out of the system

- **After you create your circulatory system, use a funnel to pour colored water into the system or pump.**

- **Pump the water so it moves through the circulatory system.** What happens? How far does the water make it around the system in a single pump? Does the water reach every part of the body? Does the water move in one direction or does it move back and forth? What would happen in the human body if blood moved in both directions? If your system were vertical, how would the force of gravity affect it?

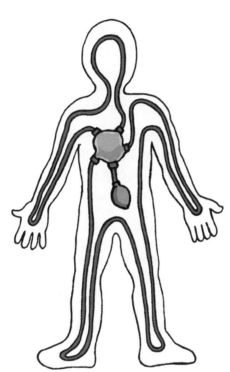

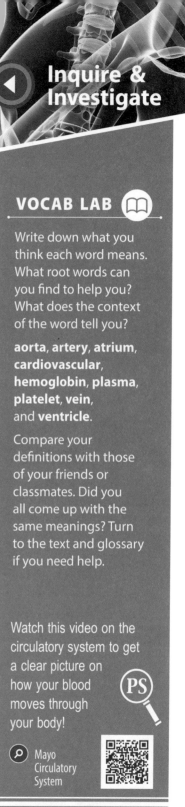

Inquire & Investigate

VOCAB LAB 📖

Write down what you think each word means. What root words can you find to help you? What does the context of the word tell you?

aorta, artery, atrium, cardiovascular, hemoglobin, plasma, platelet, vein, and **ventricle**.

Compare your definitions with those of your friends or classmates. Did you all come up with the same meanings? Turn to the text and glossary if you need help.

Watch this video on the circulatory system to get a clear picture on how your blood moves through your body!

(PS)

🔍 Mayo Circulatory System

To investigate more, think about any problems you found in your design. What changes could you make to create a more efficient circulatory system based on what you've learned? Build and test your redesign. What happens? How is it better or worse than your first design?

Ideas for Supplies ▼

- wide-mouth jar
- red food coloring
- large balloon
- 2 flexible drinking straws
- wooden skewer

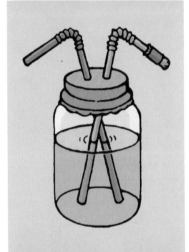

MAKE A PUMPING HEART

The heart works 24/7 to keep life-giving blood flowing to every part of the body. In this activity, you'll create your own version of one chamber in the hard-working, pumping heart.

- **Fill the jar about half full of red water.** Cut the neck off the balloon and save it for later. Stretch the balloon over the jar's opening, pulling it down as tightly as you can to make the balloon's surface as flat as possible.

- **Use a wooden skewer to carefully poke two holes in the balloon's surface.** The holes should be on directly opposite sides of the jar with about an inch between them. Push a straw snugly into each hole so no air can flow between the hole and the straw.

- **Slide the uncut end of the balloon neck that you cut off earlier onto one of the straws.** Tape it around the straw.

- **Place the jar in a large pan or a sink to catch water.** Bend the straws downward and then gently press in the center of the stretched balloon. What happens to the water in the jar? What happens to the straw with the cut end of the balloon? How does it act like a valve in the heart?

> **To investigate more,** take the balloon valve off the straw. Pump the water again. What happens this time? Why is the valve important to the heart's function?

Chapter 4 ▶
Breathe Deep: The Respiratory System

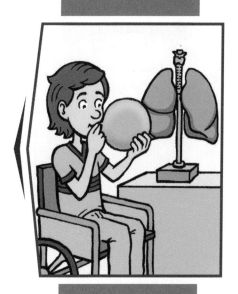

What role does the respiratory system play in a healthy body?

The lungs are responsible for getting oxygen and nutrients to the cells and organs in the body, while removing waste products such as carbon dioxide.

Take a deep breath. Now exhale. Those two simple actions are essential for life. Every time you fill your lungs with air, you bring oxygen into your body. Without oxygen, the cells throughout your body would not get the energy they need and would not survive. As you've learned, healthy cells are essential to the well-being of the entire body.

Getting the oxygen from the air into our body and our blood is the job of the respiratory system. The organs of the respiratory system—your nose, mouth, larynx, trachea, bronchi, and lungs—manage the flow of air into and out of your body.

Breathing is automatic—it's something that you do without even thinking about it.

That's good because you couldn't live without regular breathing. Let's look at how breathing works.

Have you ever seen a pair of bellows? This is a device that produces a strong blast of air, often used to supply a fire with oxygen. A simple bellows is an airtight, flexible bag with two rigid handles. When you open and expand the handles, a valve fitted on the bag allows air in. When you close the handles, the air in the bag is forcefully pushed out of the bag through a tube.

Your lungs operate like a giant pair of bellows. They draw air into the body to get oxygen. Then, they push the air in the lungs back out to expel waste carbon dioxide. An average human breathes about 12 times per minute when resting. This can increase to 20 breaths per minute or more when exercising. The act of breathing is called ventilation.

GOOD VENTILATION

When you take a breath, you draw air into the body through the nose or mouth. As air passes through the nose or mouth, it is warmed and moistened. Nasal hairs filter out dust particles that could irritate the lungs or other parts of the respiratory system.

Next, air passes down the throat to the trachea, also called the windpipe. The trachea is protected by rings of cartilage to prevent it from collapsing. From the trachea, air travels into the left or right bronchus of the lungs. The right bronchus supplies air to the right lung, while the left bronchus supplies air to the left lung.

SNORE!

Chances are you know someone who snores. It might be short grunts or loud, rumbling snores. No matter how it sounds, the anatomy of snoring is similar. When a person snores, the upper airway partially collapses. The tongue falls back and the soft palate—the fleshy, flexible part of the roof of your mouth—vibrates with each breath. The vibrating soft palate then makes air in the throat vibrate, which causes the snoring sound you hear.

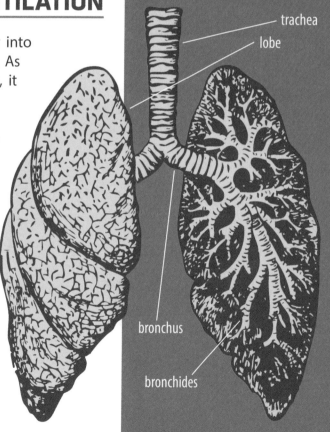

trachea
lobe
bronchus
bronchides

The average human takes about 8.5 million breaths a year!

HELP FOR ASTHMA SUFFERERS

Do you or someone you know have asthma? Asthma is the sudden constriction of lung muscles that narrows the bronchioles and causes the person to experience a shortness of breath. When a person has asthma, their airways become inflamed or constricted in reaction to certain triggers, such as temperature, particles in the air, and even stress. This makes breathing difficult. A person may cough, wheeze, or experience shortness of breath. In severe asthma, the symptoms lead to hypoxemia, which is when there is not enough oxygen in the blood.

Inside the chest, protected by the rib cage, the lungs are one of the largest organs in the body. You actually have two lungs, one on the right and one on the left. The left lung is smaller than the right in order to make room for the heart. Both lungs are separated into lobes—three on the right and two on the left. The lobes are further divided into segments and then lobules.

After traveling through the bronchi into the lungs, air continues into smaller and smaller air passages called bronchioles in each lung. The bronchioles are covered with mucus, which keeps them moist and traps any inhaled particles. Eventually, air reaches tiny, balloon-like air sacs in the lungs called alveoli.

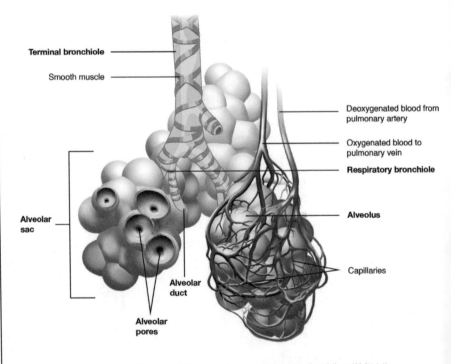

credit: Anatomy & Physiology, Connexions Website, OpenStax College (CC BY 3.0)

Beneath the lungs, the diaphragm is a dome-shaped muscle that works with the lungs when you inhale and exhale. When you breathe in, the diaphragm contracts and pulls down. As the diaphragm pulls down, it creates a vacuum that pulls air into the lungs. At the same time, the chest muscles between your ribs contract. This lifts the ribs so the lungs expand as air rushes into them. Then, the diaphragm relaxes and moves upward and pushes on the lungs. The chest muscles also relax, and the chest tightens. The lungs reduce in size and force air out of them. You exhale.

EXCHANGING GASES

The main jobs of the respiratory system are to extract oxygen from the air and to remove carbon dioxide from the body.

> Oxygen provides the energy that powers every cell, every process in the body.

Cells use oxygen to break down the sugars from food and create energy. When this happens, carbon dioxide is produced. Your blood carries the carbon dioxide back to the lungs and expels it from your body when you exhale.

This gas exchange occurs in about 300 million tiny air sacs called alveoli. The alveoli cluster together like grapes and give the lungs their sponge-like texture. Tiny blood vessels called capillaries wrap around every alveolus. Blood in the capillaries carries molecules of carbon dioxide that it has picked up from cells in the body. The walls of both alveoli and capillaries are extremely thin—each is only one cell thick. This helps the process of diffusion, during which gases are exchanged.

Thin strips of muscle line each bronchiole.

IIIIIIIIIIIIIIIIIIIIIIIIIIIIIIIIIIIIIIIIIII

MMMMMUCUS

Mucus may be gross, but it's an important part of the respiratory system. Mucus is a thick fluid that exists in the respiratory system and other body systems. Mucus is produced in the mucous membranes. These membranes have special cells and glands that secrete mucus. The average human produces about a liter of mucus per day. In your respiratory system, mucus lines the entire airway. Cilia in the bronchi and bronchioles constantly sweep the stream of mucus back up the airway toward the throat. In the nasal passage, mucus warms and moistens the air. It traps dust and irritants in its stickiness and expels them out of the body. When you get a respiratory illness such as a cold, the flu, allergies, asthma, or chronic bronchitis, extra mucus is produced. Sneezing clears the extra mucus from the upper respiratory tracts. Coughing clears it from the lower tracts.

Have you ever noticed that it is harder to breathe at a high altitude? That's because at high altitudes, the air is thinner and has less oxygen. Your body may automatically take deeper breaths because it detects that oxygen levels in the blood are lower than normal. People who travel to high altitudes can temporarily produce more red blood cells to carry more oxygen in their blood. Those who permanently live in high altitudes may adapt by developing larger lungs, wider chests, and more efficient oxygen-processing genes.

Watch this video to learn more about alveoli and gas exchange in the lungs.

Science sauce alveoli gas exchange

In diffusion, molecules move from an area of greater concentration to an area of lower concentration. Carbon dioxide molecules diffuse in the lungs from the blood plasma through the walls of the capillaries and alveoli. The lungs exhale the carbon dioxide and release it from the body.

At the same time, oxygen molecules diffuse from the alveoli into the blood plasma. The oxygen dissolves in the plasma and is taken up by the hemoglobin in red blood cells. After absorbing oxygen, the blood leaves the lungs and travels to your heart. The heart pumps the oxygen-rich blood through your body so it can deliver oxygen to the cells of organs and tissues that need it. Along the way, the blood picks up more carbon dioxide waste from cells before returning to the lungs to start the process all over again.

SAY WHAT?

Not only is the respiratory system essential for breathing, it's also important for talking.

Hold two fingers to your throat and hum. What do you feel?

Above the trachea sits the larynx, also called the voice box. Across the voice box, two tiny ridges called vocal cords open and close to make sounds. When you exhale air from your lungs, it flows through the trachea and larynx to the vocal cords. When the vocal cords are closed, the air flows between them and makes them vibrate. This produces a sound wave. The lips and tongue shape the sound waves into speech.

The amount of air expelled by the lungs determines how loud the sound is. It also determines how long you can make that sound. Try inhaling deeply and then reading a passage from this book aloud. How far can you make it without taking another breath? In a similar way, shouting loudly requires a lot of air. If you shout, you need to breathe more often than if you speak the same words softly!

HEALTHY LUNGS

Despite all the respiratory system's defenses, some irritants and other foreign particles reach the lungs. Once there, they can cause problems.

Pneumonia is an infection that causes mucus and pus to build up in the airway, making it hard to breath. Tuberculosis (TB) is an infection of the lungs caused by bacteria. In this disease, areas of the bronchial and lung tissue become inflamed and die. This leaves a hole in the tissue where air can leak. When air leaks out from the lung, it can cause the lung to collapse. Most babies get a vaccine for tuberculosis, and incidents of this disease continue to decrease.

Emphysema affects people who have had long-term exposure to lung irritants such as cigarette smoke, chemicals, asbestos, or coal. The damage to the bronchioles from decades of irritation causes them to collapse and trap air inside. The pressure of the trapped air can rupture the alveoli and destroy the respiratory tissue in that area.

Just as you want to keep your muscles and heart healthy, you want to do the same for your lungs. And, funny enough, many of the same things you do for the rest of your body helps your lungs, too!

BODY WISE

A hiccup is a quick, involuntary contraction of the diaphragm. Each contraction is followed by the sudden closing of your vocal cords, causing the sound of a hiccup. No one knows exactly why this reflex action occurs.

PANT!

Have you noticed that when you run or exercise intensely, you tend to get out of breath? Your muscles burn a lot of energy as you exercise. This quickly uses up the oxygen in your body's red blood cells. To get more energy and oxygen to the muscles, your heart pumps faster to get more blood into the lungs. At the same time, the lungs try to breathe faster and deeper to get more oxygen.

Personal Filtering System

The respiratory system has built-in systems to prevent harmful substances in the air from entering the lungs. In the nose, hairs filter out large particles. Tiny, microscopic hairs called cilia line your air passages. The cilia constantly move in a sweeping motion and carry foreign matter upward for swallowing or to be expelled to keep the passages clean. Cells in the trachea and bronchial tubes produce mucus that keeps the air passage moist and also traps dust, bacteria, viruses, allergens, and other particles before they enter the lungs. Coughing can expel particles that manage to reach the lungs. All of this is meant to keep you healthy!

TEXT TO WORLD

Do you know anyone who smokes? What effect does that have on their health? On yours?

The main tool at your disposal is one of prevention—don't smoke or vape. Smoking leads to disastrous effect on your respiratory system, including lung disease and, eventually, death. Vaping can have the same or similar affects as smoking.

Other things in your control are exercising regularly, eating healthfully, and keeping your own environment free from dust and other irritants.

Regular exercise strengthens the lungs. Over time, your body becomes more efficient at getting oxygen into the bloodstream and delivering it the body. Aerobic activities such as walking or running give your lungs the workout they need to get stronger. Muscle-strengthening exercise such as weight-lifting builds core strength and tones breathing muscles, allowing you to breathe more deeply and effectively.

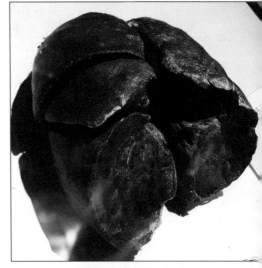

The blackened lungs of a cigarette smoke
credit: David Jackmanson (CC BY 2.

KEY QUESTIONS

- Why is chemical exchange crucial for a healthy body?
- Why might the same methods that keep the circulatory system healthy keep the respiratory working well, too?

TEST THE EFFECTS OF EXERCISE ON BREATHING

The body uses oxygen to burn the fuel in your cells to produce energy. Through breathing, the lungs pull oxygen from the air into the body and expel carbon dioxide. Red blood cells transport oxygen to all the body's tissues and cells. In this experiment, you will test how exercise affects our breathing.

- **Gather several volunteers and have them sit quietly at rest for five minutes.** Measure their breaths per minute and pulse while resting. Record the measurements.

- **Measure each volunteer's lung capacity.** You can do this by having each person take a deep breath and blow it all out into a balloon. Measure and record the circumference of the balloon. What does this estimate?

- **Have each person stand and do jumping jacks for 30 seconds and have them count and record how many jumping jacks they completed in that time.** Immediately after the jumping jacks, measure and record their breaths per minute and pulse.

- **Create a graph or chart to summarize and compare the data you collected.** What observations did you make about your volunteers' breathing? How did exercise affect breathing? How did exercise affect heart rate? Why do you think this happened? Was there a correlation between lung capacity and breathing rate?

VOCAB LAB

Write down what you think each word means. What root words can you find to help you? What does the context of the word tell you?

alveoli, **bronchus**, **diaphragm**, **larynx**, **mucus**, **reflex action**, and **trachea**.

Compare your definitions with those of your friends or classmates. Did you all come up with the same meanings? Turn to the text and glossary if you need help.

To investigate more, repeat this experiment with volunteers of different ages, or athletes vs. non-athletes. What observations do you have? How do the variables of age and physical condition affect breathing?

Chapter 5

Command Central: The Nervous System

How does your body know when to react and what to do?

The nervous system, which includes your brain, is a highly sophisticated system that your body uses to sense the surrounding or internal environments and develop a reaction to those environments. Your nervous system keeps you alive!

How does your body know what to do in different situations? Imagine that you are at a swim meet. You line up with the other swimmers on the starting blocks. When the buzzer sounds, you dive off the block and swim toward the other end of the pool as fast as you can. Your arms move, your legs kick, and your head turns to take a breath.

How does your body know what actions to take? That's the job of the nervous system. It's the body's command central. The nervous system directs how the body operates and controls the flow of information within the body.

The nervous system allows you to experience the world around you and to respond to it. A ball flies in the air toward you and you reach up to catch it. The smell of cupcakes baking in the oven makes your mouth water. All these actions and reactions occur because of the work of your nervous system.

Through a complex network of nerves and cells, the nervous system carries messages throughout the body and controls its actions.

The nervous system has three main jobs. First, it collects information about what is going on inside and outside your body through special sensory receptors. It sends this information to either the spinal cord or the brain. Second, the nervous system interprets the information it receives. Finally, it sends a response to different parts of the body.

The structures of your nervous system reach into every organ in your body. They are involved in one way or another in nearly every physiological reaction. From playing with your dog to digesting your lunch, each action involves the nervous system. For example, when your friend throws the ball at you, your eyes see the ball, your brain tells your arms to reach for it, and your hands catch it. That's your nervous system at work.

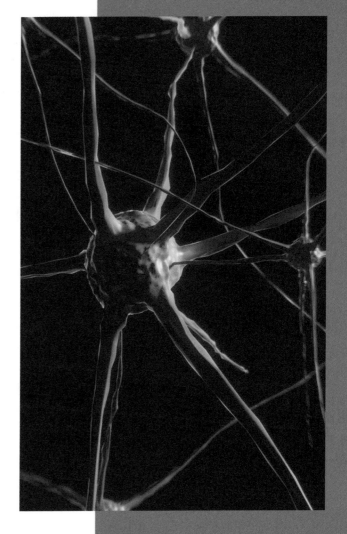

(ALMOST) INSTANT MESSENGER

How does the nervous system send messages throughout the body? It starts with specialized cells called neurons. Neurons are unlike any other cell in the body. Neurons send electrical signals, which cause the sensations, movement, and thoughts that you have. The human nervous system has billions of neurons.

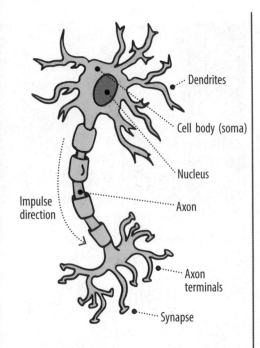

Dendrites

Cell body (soma)

Nucleus

Axon

Impulse direction

Axon terminals

Synapse

Although neurons come in many shapes and sizes, most have the same basic structure. The neuron's cell body, called a soma, contains its nucleus. Together, they maintain the cell and keep the neuron functioning. The soma connects to dendrites, which stretch out from the cell like the branches of a tree.

Dendrites receive chemical messages from other neurons. Here's how. When a signal comes into a neuron from one of its dendrites, a chemical reaction begins in its nucleus, which causes electrical activity. If enough signals are received, a tiny blast called an action potential, or nerve impulse, travels to the neuron's axon, a thin nerve fiber that conducts electrical signals, and enters the axon terminal.

The axon terminal fires the electrical signal across a gap between nerve cells—this gap is called a synapse. A synapse separates one neuron's axon from the dendrites of another neuron. The signal is carried across the synapse by a chemical substance called a neurotransmitter. The neurotransmitter moves across the space and attaches to receptors on the dendrites of a nearby neuron. The next neuron sends the message from its dendrites down to its cell body and the process continues.

Some axons are short and send signals from one neuron in the cortex to another neuron only a tiny distance away. Other axons are very long and carry signals from the brain down the spinal cord.

The nervous system has three types of neurons: motor, sensory, and interneuron. Motor neurons send information between organs, muscles, and glands, and are responsible for controlling muscles. Sensory neurons collect information from inside and outside the body and send it to the brain and spinal cord so you can react to different stimuli. Interneurons are messengers that transmit information between motor and sensory neurons. You need all three to function!

Unlike other cells in the body, neurons don't touch each other. They are separated by spaces called synapses. To communicate, neurons send signals across the synapses by firing a chemical from one neuron to the next.

COMMUNICATION NETWORK

When neurons send signals, they travel through the nervous system to other parts of the brain and body through a network of neurons. The nervous system has two main networks. The central nervous system (CNS) includes the brain and the spinal cord. The peripheral nervous system (PNS) is a complex network of nerves that spread through the body.

The CNS and PNS work together to send information throughout the body.

If you want to move your leg, your brain sends a message down the spinal cord to the PNS that tells your leg to move.

Messages are sent back to the brain the same way. Sensory input travels from receptor points throughout the body through the PNS to the brain. The brain processes and interprets the information in a fraction of a second, then makes a decision, which is sent through the PNS to the muscles, which take the needed action, such as making sure that leg is high enough now to reach the next step.

CENTRAL NERVOUS SYSTEM

As you think, see, breathe, and move throughout the day, you use your CNS. The CNS receives and processes all the information from every part of your body. The main functions of the CNS are to process sensory information and determine the appropriate reaction. The CNS is one of the most important systems in your body.

Sensory neurons let you know how close to the fireplace to sit!

BODY WISE

Twelve pairs of cranial nerves transmit motor or sensory signals between the brain or brain stem and the head and neck.

Watch an animation of how neurons exchange messages in this video.

 medical net nervous system

The brain contains billions of nerve cells whose workings make it the most complex organ in the body.

The brain is the main organ of the nervous system and serves as the body's control center—it coordinates all body functions. It receives information from all parts of your body, as well as from the outside world. The brain processes and interprets this information, creating the sights, sounds, thoughts, and actions you experience. The brain is also responsible for keeping your body alive by regulating your heart rate, keeping you breathing, and controlling other essential functions. That's a lot of responsibility!

The brain is divided into three main sections: the cerebrum, cerebellum, and brain stem. The cerebrum is the large wrinkled structure that sits at the uppermost part of the brain. Higher mental processing takes place in the cerebrum. The cerebrum also controls voluntary muscles—the ones that move when you want them to move. When you plan a get-together with your friends, read books, or learn a new language, you are using parts of the cerebrum. Your memories are stored in the cerebrum. The cerebrum also aids in reasoning, helping you decide whether it is better to do your homework now or later.

The cerebrum is divided into two halves, the right and left hemispheres, that work together. The two hemispheres are physically linked by a large bundle of nerves—about 200 million densely packed nerve cells—called the corpus callosum. The two hemispheres communicate by sending messages through the corpus callosum.

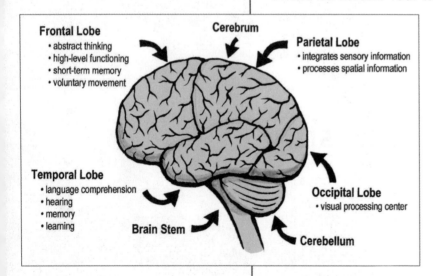

Frontal Lobe
• abstract thinking
• high-level functioning
• short-term memory
• voluntary movement

Cerebrum

Parietal Lobe
• integrates sensory information
• processes spatial information

Temporal Lobe
• language comprehension
• hearing
• memory
• learning

Brain Stem

Occipital Lobe
• visual processing center

Cerebellum

The hemispheres of the brain are covered with a layer of tissue about 3 millimeters thick. This layer is called the cerebral cortex. Most of the brain's information processing occurs in the cortex.

The cerebellum is located at the back of the brain, below the cerebrum. Although it is much smaller than the cerebrum, the cerebellum controls several important functions, including body movement, balance, and posture. When you kick a ball or play the piano, the cerebellum is involved. Without the cerebellum, you would not be able to stand upright or balance on one foot.

Underneath the cerebrum and in front of the cerebellum, the brain stem connects the brain to the spinal cord. The brain stem keeps you alive. It is responsible for many of the body's most basic functions, such as breathing and circulating blood. The brain stem also controls involuntary muscles, which move without you even deciding on it. Your heart and stomach work with involuntary muscles. The brain stem tells the heart to beat fast or the stomach to digest food. The brain stem also acts as a relay station for the millions of messages that are sent between the brain and body.

The other main organ of the CNS, the spinal cord, is a bundle of nerve fibers that connects the base of the brain and runs down your back. The spinal cord transmits information from all over your body to the brain for processing. It also sends messages from the brain back to every part of the body.

Check out the different things controlled by the left and right hemispheres of the brain!

 neuroscience for kids Washington

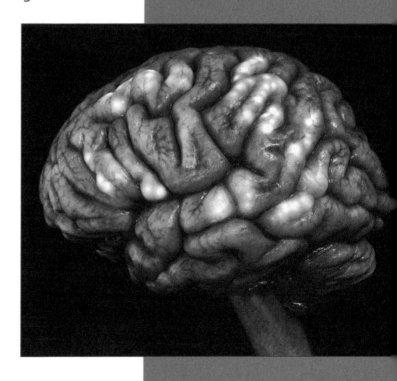

REFLEX ACTION

At your annual physical, the doctor taps your knee with a small hammer. Your leg automatically jerks in response, even though you didn't move it intentionally. This is an example of a reflex action—an involuntary movement the body makes in response to a stimulus. Another example is the dilation of the pupils in your eyes to adjust to less light. Your brain does not control these automatic reactions to stimuli. Instead, the spinal cord receives the information about the stimuli and quickly sends a response to your body. Reflexes often protect you from things that can hurt you. For example, if you touch something hot, you quickly pull your hand back without thinking about it. That's a reflex action. Sensory nerves in your hand transmit signals about the heat to the spinal cord. The neurons in the spinal cord immediately transmit signals back to motor neurons in your hand's muscles to trigger the reflex to pull your hand away.

PERIPHERAL NERVOUS SYSTEM

The PNS includes all the nerves that travel to and from the CNS. The PNS is like a system of wires throughout your body. The nerves of the PNS gather sensory information and report it to the brain and spinal cord. These messages tell the brain what is happening inside and outside your body. The CNS processes this information and sends orders back to the PNS. The PNS carries these orders to the body's organs, limbs, and skin. It causes the body to react to what is going on around it. The PNS is the body's message delivery system.

The PNS has two main types of nerves. Sensory nerves carry messages from the sensory organs, such as your skin, eyes, ears, nose, and tongue, to the CNS. Motor nerves carry orders from the CNS to the body's muscles and organs.

The PNS has two parts: the somatic system and the autonomic system. The somatic nervous system carries sensory and motor information to and from the CNS. Sensory neurons take in information and send it to the CNS. Motor neurons carry information from the CNS to muscle fibers throughout the body. This allows your body to move in response to stimuli in the environment.

Imagine that you are walking your dog on a winter morning. You spot a patch of slick-looking ice on the sidewalk ahead of you. Your eyes and visual sensory system see the icy patch and send this information to the brain. Your brain processes it and sends signals via the nerve networks of the somatic system to your muscles to take action. Your body reacts and you step to the side and walk on a different part of the path. Thanks to the somatic nervous system!

The autonomic system is the part of the PNS that keeps the body working even when you are not telling it to do anything.

For example, the autonomic system tells your stomach to digest food and your lungs to breathe. These activities happen without you having to think about them. The autonomic system controls several body processes, including digestion, blood pressure, heart rate, and body temperature.

The autonomic system is made up of three main parts: the sympathetic nervous system, parasympathetic nervous system, and enteric nervous system.

- **The sympathetic nervous system** responds to stress and is responsible for the body's fight-or-flight response. It prepares the body to act when it perceives a potential threat. The sympathetic system speeds up the heart rate, increases the breathing rate, increases blood flow to the muscles, activates sweat secretion, and dilates the pupils. This allows the body to respond quickly—either to fight the threat or flee from it.

- **The parasympathetic nervous system** helps the body maintain normal body functions. Once a threat has passed, the parasympathetic system returns the body to its normal resting state. It slows the heart rate, slows breathing, reduces blood flow to the muscles, and constricts the pupils.

- **The enteric nervous system** helps the body with the process of digestion. You will learn about the digestive system in Chapter 7.

BODY WISE

Your body has 31 pairs of spinal nerves. Each spinal nerve contains sensory and motor neurons that carry messages to and from various parts of your body.

EPILEPSY

Epilepsy is a nervous system disorder that occurs when the electrical communication between the brain's neurons gets disrupted and causes a person to have a seizure. A seizure is a change in a person's behavior caused by abnormal electrical activity in the brain. A seizure may cause a person to fall down, shake, stiffen, throw up, or pass out. Other seizures are less noticeable. A person might just be still and stare into space or have jerking movements in one part of the body. After a seizure, a person may not remember what happened. Some people with epilepsy have only occasional seizures, while others have several seizures each day.

What about pain? The nervous system reacts to pain stimuli in interesting ways. Take a look at this TED talk on how we feel with pain. It might be more complex than you think!

 TED Joshua Pate pain

BODY WISE

The electrical activity generated by nerve cells can be seen on some brain scans. By looking at these scans, scientists can see which areas of the brain are active during different activities.

TEXT TO WORLD

Do you have one sense that is stronger or weaker than your other senses? How does that affect how your brain gets information about the environment?

SENSING YOUR ENVIRONMENT

How does your body get information from the outside world to send to the brain? Your senses! Through sight, hearing, taste, touch, and smell, your senses collect information about the world around you. This information is sent via the nervous system to the brain, which processes it and sends signals for the appropriate action and reaction.

Your body has several sense organs. The eyes, ears, skin, nose, and tongue receive stimuli such as light and sound and pressure. The sense organs have receptors that transform stimuli into electrical signals and send them to specialized areas of the brain's cerebral cortex. Here, they are processed into sensations.

The light that hits your eye becomes the sight of a friend. The vibrations that entered your ear become your friend's voice.

Our senses are constantly gathering information and sending it to the brain. Another system helps send and receive messages throughout the body. We'll learn about the endocrine system in the next chapter.

KEY QUESTIONS

- **What is the difference between the autonomic nervous system and the somatic nervous system?**
- **How does a neuron receive and send messages?**

BUILD A NEURON

The neuron is the worker of the nervous system. This specialized cell transmits nerve impulses that allow the brain and nervous system to communicate. Each part of a neuron's structure plays a role in the neuron's overall function. In this activity, you will build a neuron to better understand how it functions.

- **Research the neuron's structure and function.** You can look at microscopic slides of real neurons here. science week neuron gallery

- **Draw a design of a model of a neuron.** Label each structure in the neuron.

- **Gather a variety of materials, such as pipe cleaners, modeling clay, beads, string, paint and brushes, newspaper, Styrofoam balls, or other items.**

- **Select some materials and build a model neuron.** Make sure that you include the dendrites, cell body, nucleus, axon, and axon terminals in the model. What is the function of dendrites? What is the function of axon terminals?

- **Use the model to explain the structure and function of a neuron to your friends or classmates.** Why is it important to understand the structure and function of a neuron? How did the model help you to explain? In what ways could you improve the neuron model?

VOCAB LAB 📖

Write down what you think each word means. What root words can you find to help you? What does the context of the word tell you?

central nervous system, **cerebrum**, **cerebellum**, **dendrite**, **neuron**, **peripheral nervous system**, and **synapse**.

Compare your definitions with those of your friends or classmates. Did you all come up with the same meanings? Turn to the text and glossary if you need help.

To investigate more, add more neurons to your model and demonstrate how a nerve signal passes from one neuron to the next. What happens if something goes wrong with a neuron and its ability to pass a signal?

A TEST OF NERVES

How do you know when something touches your arm or someone taps you on the shoulder? Neurons in the peripheral nervous system sense stimuli such as touch and send a signal to the brain. Each neuron can send only one message at a time. If two things touch you and activate the same neuron, it can still send only one signal to the brain. When this happens, the brain senses only one thing touching you, instead of two. Do you think that every part of the body has the same number of nerves? Which parts do you think have a lot of nerves? Why?

- **Select three different parts of your body.** Which part do you think will be the most sensitive? Which do you think will be the least sensitive? Why?

- **To test your prediction, open a large paper clip.** Spread the ends until they are exactly 4 centimeters apart. Gently touch the first body part with both ends of the paper clip. Do you feel both ends? Or do you feel only one end? Record your response. Repeat this step on the other body parts you are testing.

- **Adjust the paper clip so that the ends are 3 centimeters apart.** Repeat the testing on the body parts. Then, repeat the test with the paper clip ends at 2 centimeters apart, 1 centimeter apart, and touching. Record your results.

- **Organize your results in a chart or graph.** Which part of the body was the least sensitive? Which was the most sensitive? Why do you think this occurred? Do your results support your hypothesis?

To investigate more, try testing additional body parts or changing the stimulus from a paper clip to a different object. How does this affect your results? What further questions does this raise and how could you design an experiment to investigate those questions?

Chapter 6 ▶

Chemical Messages: The Endocrine System

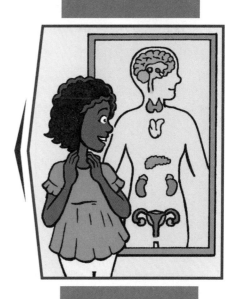

What does the endocrine system do in your body?

The glands and organs that make up the endocrine system release chemicals that prompt different feelings and behaviors. It's hormones that make you feel sad or happy, hungry or full.

Have you ever heard someone blame behavior on hormones? This happens pretty frequently with teenagers, since adolescence is a time when bodies are going through a lot of hormonal change. Hormones are chemical substances that travel throughout the body in your blood. They trigger changes that regulate everything from your mood and sleep to growth and development. Organs called glands secrete hormones. Together, they are the body's endocrine system.

While the nervous system controls faster processes such as breathing and heartbeat, the endocrine system controls body processes, such as cell growth, that happen during a longer period of time. The nervous system and the endocrine system often work closely together. For example, the nervous system controls the timing of what the endocrine system does.

Let's take a closer look at the endocrine system.

WHAT IS A HORMONE?

Hormones act as chemical messengers to the body's organs and tissues. They give cells instructions to keep the body in balance or to bring about long-term changes, such as growth. After being released by glands into the blood, hormones travel via the circulatory system throughout the body.

Hormones do not affect every cell, just cells that have specific receptors to receive them. Each hormone has a specific shape and can bind only to a matching receptor. If the cell does not have the right receptor, the hormone does not bind to it and has no effect. Cells can have between 5,000 and 100,000 hormone receptors.

In some cells, receptors float in the cell's cytoplasm. Hormones pass through the outer membrane of a target cell and bind to the receptors. Together, the receptors and hormones cross into the nucleus of the cell.

Inside the nucleus, the receptor-hormone pair binds to the cell's DNA and activates a specific gene. For example, estrogen is a hormone produced by the female ovaries. It targets certain body cells and passes through the cell membranes. Inside the cells, estrogen binds to the estrogen-specific receptors. Together, they enter the cell nucleus. There, estrogen activates a gene to make a specific protein. This protein in turn makes oxytocin, which prepares the female body for childbirth.

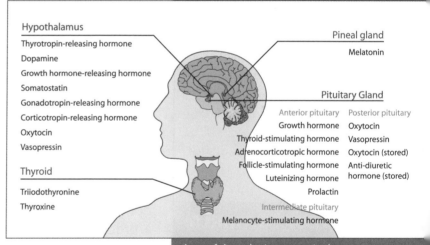

Hypothalamus
Thyrotropin-releasing hormone
Dopamine
Growth hormone-releasing hormone
Somatostatin
Gonadotropin-releasing hormone
Corticotropin-releasing hormone
Oxytocin
Vasopressin

Thyroid
Triiodothyronine
Thyroxine

Pineal gland
Melatonin

Pituitary Gland

Anterior pituitary	Posterior pituitary
Growth hormone	Oxytocin
Thyroid-stimulating hormone	Vasopressin
Adrenocorticotropic hormone	Oxytocin (stored)
Follicle-stimulating hormone	Anti-diuretic
Luteinizing hormone	hormone (stored)
Prolactin	

Intermediate pituitary
Melanocyte-stimulating hormone

Areas of the endocrine system in the head and neck

Other hormones do not pass through the cell membrane. Instead, these hormones bind to receptors that line the cell's surface. They trigger the cell to make a second messenger protein, which causes additional changes in the cell.

WHAT CAUSES HORMONES?

What triggers glands to secrete hormones in the first place? Sometimes, nerve signals trigger the release of hormones.

Have you ever seen a growling dog? When you encounter a threat, your nervous system sends a signal to your adrenal gland. This causes secretion of a hormone called epinephrine. Epinephrine plays an important role in your body's fight-or-flight response to a threat. Within seconds, epinephrine binds with target cells to increase blood flow to your muscles, dilate your pupils, increase your heart rate, and increase your blood sugar levels. These body changes prepare you to run or fight.

Hormones can also be triggered when sensory cells detect changes in your blood and other body fluids. For example, calcium is essential to strong and healthy bones. If sensory cells detect low calcium levels, the parathyroid gland releases parathyroid hormone (PTH). PTH plays a role in bone remodeling, a process in which old bone tissue is absorbed by the body and new bone is built.

Sometimes, one hormone can trigger the release of another hormone. The hypothalamus gland produces several hormones that control other glands, including the pituitary gland. When the hypothalamus produces a growth hormone-releasing hormone, this hormone travels to the pituitary gland to trigger the release of growth hormone. Growth hormone stimulates growth, cell reproduction, and cell regeneration in the body.

KEEPING THE BODY IN BALANCE

Hormones and the endocrine system play important roles in homeostasis, the process of keeping the body in balance. Glands release hormones in response to information gathered in the body in a feedback loop.

As the blood passes through certain checkpoints in the nervous system, receptors measure hormone levels. If the level of a certain hormone is too low, the gland that produces the hormone is triggered to secrete more of it. If the hormone level is too high, the gland that produces it either stops secreting the hormone or slows production.

While the endocrine system produces the hormones, the nervous system gives the directions on when to secrete those hormones.

Let's take a look at how this feedback loop works to keep the body in balance. What happens when the parathyroid gland detects low levels of calcium in the blood? Calcium is one of the most abundant minerals in the human body. It is essential for bone and teeth formation. It's important for the body to have the right levels of calcium in the blood.

The checkpoints in the nervous system also monitor a variety of body conditions, such as temperature, glucose level, or pH level. If any of these conditions become too low or too high, the nervous system and endocrine system work together to manage hormone levels to bring the body back into balance.

|||||||||||||||||||||||||||||||||||||||||

These are foods rich in calcium

In response to low levels of calcium, the parathyroid glands release parathyroid hormone (PTH). PTH stimulates cells in the bones called osteoclasts to break down bone tissue, which releases calcium into the blood. It also signals the gut to start absorbing more calcium from food. Back in balance!

What happens if calcium levels swing the other way and are now too high in the blood? When the thyroid gland detects high levels of calcium in the blood, it produces the hormone calcitonin. Calcitonin stimulates cells in the bone called osteoblasts to use calcium in the blood to build bone tissue. At the same time, the parathyroid stops producing PTH. Without PTH, the osteoclasts in bone stop breaking down bone tissue and releasing calcium into the blood. The body's calcium levels return to a normal state.

In this way, the endocrine system jumps back into action to reduce those levels and bring the body back into balance.

BODY WISE

Some organs carry out several functions in the body and have roles in multiple organ systems. For example, the pancreas plays a part in both the endocrine and digestive systems.

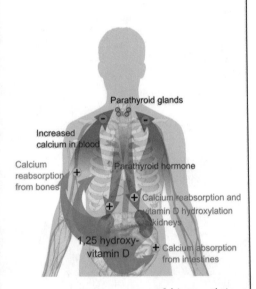

Parathyroid glands

Increased calcium in blood

Calcium reabsorption from bones

Parathyroid hormone

Calcium reabsorption and vitamin D hydroxylation in kidneys

1,25 hydroxy-vitamin D

Calcium absorption from intestines

Calcium regulation

WHERE DO HORMONES COME FROM?

Hormones are made in glands and organs throughout the body. Some organs of the endocrine system only produce hormones, while other organs, such as the stomach or kidneys, have other functions, too. The major parts of the endocrine system include:

- **Pituitary gland**—controls the growth and development of tissues and the function of other endocrine glands

- **Thyroid gland**—regulates growth and metabolism

- **Parathyroid glands**—regulate calcium levels in the blood and bones

- **Adrenal glands**—produce hormones that regulate the fight-or-flight response, blood pressure, and metabolism

- **Pancreas**—produces hormones that control blood glucose levels, along with producing digestive enzymes

- **Thymus**—produces a hormone that stimulates the immune system

- **Pineal gland**—releases the hormone melatonin, which makes you sleepy

- **Ovaries**—secrete hormones that regulate female reproductive health

- **Testes**—secrete the hormone testosterone, which plays a role in male physical development

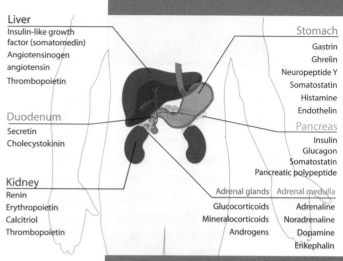

Liver
Insulin-like growth factor (somatomedin)
Angiotensinogen angiotensin
Thrombopoietin

Duodenum
Secretin
Cholecystokinin

Kidney
Renin
Erythropoietin
Calcitriol
Thrombopoietin

Stomach
Gastrin
Ghrelin
Neuropeptide Y
Somatostatin
Histamine
Endothelin

Pancreas
Insulin
Glucagon
Somatostatin
Pancreatic polypeptide

Adrenal glands | Adrenal medulla
Glucocorticoids | Adrenaline
Mineralocorticoids | Noradrenaline
Androgens | Dopamine
| Enkephalin

Areas of the endocrine system in the abdomen

Hormones are also produced by organs in the body. For example, when you eat a lot and your stomach is full, cells in the stomach lining secrete the hormone gastrin. This hormone stimulates other cells in the stomach to secrete gastric acid, which is needed to break down and digest food. When blood pressure is high, the heart secretes hormones that stimulate the kidneys to expel more water. This reduces the volume of blood in the body, which in turn decreases blood pressure.

DAILY CYCLES

Have you ever wondered why you get sleepy around the same time every day? Or why your stomach growls around the time you usually eat dinner? Part of the answer lies in your hormones.

BODY WISE

The hypothalamus, a structure in the brain, links the nervous system to the endocrine system. The hypothalamus controls thirst, fatigue, and body temperature. It also controls the hormones that make you feel excited, angry, or sad.

What happens if you sit around and spend a lot of time in front of television, computer, and phone screens? You may experience sleep problems. When exposed to the screens' bright displays late at night, your body can reduce melatonin production, the hormone that helps you sleep.

Your body has a built-in, time-keeping system that drives your daily cycle—particularly for sleeping and eating. This approximately 24-hour cycle is called a circadian rhythm. Circadian rhythms are physical, mental, and behavioral changes that follow a daily cycle. They influence your sleep-wake cycles, hormone release, eating habits, body temperature, and other body functions.

The body's circadian rhythm is controlled by a structure called the suprachiasmatic nucleus (SCN), which is a tiny area of the hypothalamus in the brain. The SCN receives information about light from the optic nerves. At night, when there is less light, the SCN tells the brain to make more of the hormone melatonin, which makes you sleepy. When the morning light stimulates the SCN, it tells the brain to convert melatonin into serotonin, which wakes up the brain.

As the day progresses, decreasing light levels trigger the conversion of serotonin into melatonin. Around midnight, melatonin levels in the blood reach their highest levels.

The hormone cortisol fluctuates during the day to help your body deal with stress. It surges in the morning and increases blood sugar levels and kick-starts your metabolism for the day. Around noon, another surge of cortisol occurs. The rest of the day, cortisol levels decline until they reach their lowest levels around midnight so that the body can rest overnight.

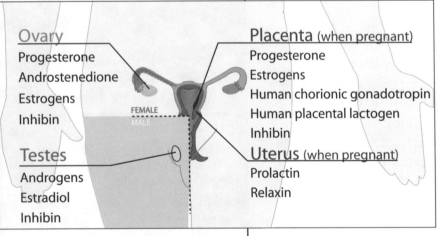

Ovary
Progesterone
Androstenedione
Estrogens
Inhibin

FEMALE
MALE

Testes
Androgens
Estradiol
Inhibin

Placenta (when pregnant)
Progesterone
Estrogens
Human chorionic gonadotropin
Human placental lactogen
Inhibin

Uterus (when pregnant)
Prolactin
Relaxin

The endocrine reproduction system

HORMONES AND HEALTH

Hormones can have a serious impact on your health. For example, being a couch potato and eating a diet full of unhealthy junk food can cause hormone changes that are harmful to your body. Physical activity triggers the release of "feel good" hormones in your body. If you are sedentary, you have fewer "feel good" hormones, which can lead you to make poor food choices. Eating a lot of junk food can cause your body to produce more of the hormone insulin to regulate blood sugar. Higher insulin levels cause the body to store fat instead of burning it.

Poor diet and inactivity can also lead to high cortisol levels. While cortisol is effective at reducing inflammation in the body, high levels during a long period can suppress the immune system. When this happens, your body isn't able to fight infection as well and it's more likely that you get sick.

On the other hand,
a healthy lifestyle can affect
hormone levels in a positive way.

Regular exercise is one of the most effective ways to trigger hormone changes that keep you healthy. Many of the hormones that prepare the body for exercise by regulating temperature, maintaining water balance, and adapting to increased oxygen demands are also "feel-good" hormones that improve your mood.

In the next chapter, we'll continue our tour inside the human body and take a look at how what you eat reaches all the way to the smallest cells!

Take a Crash Course look at the endocrine system!

 Crash Course endocrine

TEXT TO WORLD

What is your own natural circadian rhythm when it comes to sleep?

KEY QUESTIONS

- **What is the relationship between hormones and hunger? Hormones and sleep?**

- **Why is it important for calcium levels to be in balance in your body? How does the endocrine system make this happen?**

Inquire & Investigate

To investigate more, explore the latest studies on your disorder. What types of new treatments are scientists developing? How do they hope these will work? Do they believe they will be able to cure the disorder one day? Explain.

RESEARCH AN ENDOCRINE DISORDER

The endocrine system is an important part of the body because it produces and regulates hormones. When the endocrine system doesn't work correctly, this can lead to serious problems with growth, mood, and more. By learning about what can go wrong with the endocrine system, you can understand the importance of the endocrine system better. In this activity, you will choose a disorder of the endocrine system and investigate it.

- **What different types of disorders can occur in the endocrine system?** Make a list of at least five disorders. Select one of these disorders to learn more about.

- **Research your chosen disorder.** Why does it occur? What function of the endocrine system is not working properly? What glands, organs, and hormones are involved? What is the effect on the body? What problems does this cause in a person's daily life? Is this disorder temporary or permanent? What is the treatment for this disorder? How does the treatment work?

- **Create a PowerPoint or other type of presentation to explain the disorder, how it impacts the endocrine system, and its effect on the body.** Share the presentation with your class. Why is learning about disorders of body systems such as the endocrine system a good way to better understand how and why the system functions?

Chapter 7 ▶

Break It Down: The Digestive System

How does food become energy?

Your digestive system breaks down food in various ways and uses the basic nutrients in the food to power your body. Anything from the food that isn't useful gets expelled out of the body!

What's your favorite food? Pizza, spaghetti, steak, chocolate, ice cream? Do you love the way it tastes? While great taste is a definite plus, it's not the main reason why we eat. Although the body can manufacture some of the vital chemicals it needs to function, many of the building blocks the body needs are found in food.

How do you turn a piece of pepperoni pizza into something the body's cells can use? That's the job of the digestive system. The digestive system is a group of organs, passageways, and glands that work together to process the food you eat and turn it into the simple molecules that your body needs.

The digestive system includes your mouth, teeth, esophagus, stomach, small and large intestines, and rectum.

FIRST STOP: CHEWING!

To see how the process of digestion works in the body, let's follow a piece of pizza. It smells pretty good, so you take a bite. You use your teeth to chew the pizza and break it down into smaller parts. Chewing food makes it easier to swallow. It also increases the surface area of the food, which helps the digestive process later.

While you chew, salivary glands in your cheeks and under the jaw and tongue release saliva, which mixes in with the pizza. Saliva contains enzymes that break down the cell walls of food. These enzymes start breaking the complex carbohydrates in the pizza into simpler carbohydrates and sugars. Bet you didn't know that saliva was good for something other than spitting!

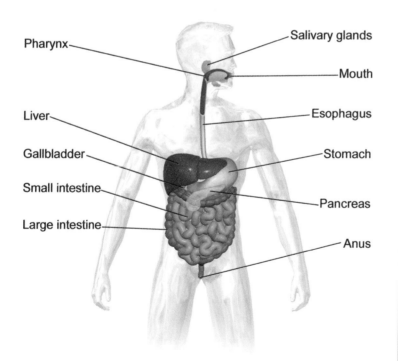

Pharynx

Liver

Gallbladder

Small intestine

Large intestine

Salivary glands

Mouth

Esophagus

Stomach

Pancreas

Anus

The components of the digestive system

HUNGRY?

You have probably felt that empty, gnawing pain in the pit of your stomach. It means you're hungry! Did you know that hormones control the feeling of hunger? When the body is low on nutrients, the stomach releases the hormone ghrelin. This hormone sends a signal to the brain, which readies the gut for food. It also causes you to feel hungry. Once you have eaten enough, fat tissues in the body release the hormone leptin. This hormone signals the brain to shut down the gut and reduce your appetite. This is one example of different body systems working together to keep you healthy.

CELIAC DISEASE

Celiac disease is a serious digestive disorder. Celiac disease occurs when the body's immune system attacks itself when gluten is present. Gluten is a protein found in grains such as wheat, barley, and rye. The immune attack damages the lining of the small intestine and harms its ability to absorb nutrients. If untreated, celiac disease can completely destroy the small intestine's villi, meaning the small intestine can't do the job of breaking down food and absorbing the nutrients.

BODY WISE

Vomiting helps the body avoid digestive problems. When you eat something rotten, the stomach, diaphragm, and abdominal muscles contract and force the food back up the esophagus and out your mouth.

Once you've chewed the pizza enough, you swallow it. It passes from the mouth down the throat through a tube called the esophagus. Gravity propels food down the esophagus, while muscular contractions in the esophagus also push the food to your stomach. A muscle outside the stomach forces it inside the stomach, even if you are lying down or standing on your head!

INTO THE STOMACH

When the pizza arrives in the stomach, the real work begins. The stomach contains strong acids and enzymes to break down food. These acids are so strong that a layer of mucus lines the stomach to protect it from its own digestive acids.

Layers of muscle in the stomach wall pull in three directions and churn the food in the digestive juices like clothes in a washing machine. The pizza stays in your stomach for a few hours, until it has a liquid or creamy consistency. It is then gradually squirted into the small intestine.

SMALL AND LARGE INTESTINES

After passing through the stomach, the pizza enters your small intestine, which is a long, thin tube that winds and snakes around your lower abdomen. In the small intestine, the pizza mixes with bile and other enzymes produced by the liver and pancreas that further break down the food into simple molecules such as glucose, amino acids, simple fatty acids, vitamins, and minerals. The walls of the small intestine are lined with thousands of fingerlike projections called villi, which absorb these molecules and move them into your blood.

The villi increase the intestine's surface area, which allows it to absorb more nutrients. Most of the nutrients in the pizza are absorbed in the small intestine.

Once in the blood, nutrients travel to the liver for processing. Meanwhile, muscular contractions in the intestine wall propel the food through the small intestine. The entire process takes three to six hours.

After traveling through the small intestine, what's left of the pizza continues to the large intestine. The large intestine is a thicker tube that winds over the small intestine and then connects to the rectum. The walls of the large intestine absorb the water in food and a few other nutrients and salts. Only the indigestible parts of the pizza remain and become a waste product. In the large intestine, waste products dry out and are pressed to form feces.

It's a long, slow process—the pizza can take 24 to 36 hours to travel through the large intestine. Once it does . . . it's time for the bathroom. And out comes the waste product through the anus!

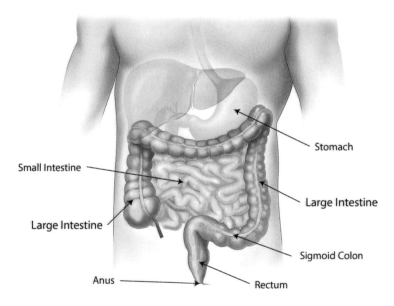

Stomach

Small Intestine

Large Intestine

Large Intestine

Sigmoid Colon

Anus

Rectum

 Watch it happen! Follow the path of your food in this video.

 Merck Manual digestive system

Don't Choke While Eating

You use your mouth to both breathe and eat. How does the body know to send food to the stomach and air to the lungs? The body has a built-in safety valve called the epiglottis that keeps food going down the "right pipe." The epiglottis is a small flap of cartilage in the throat. When you have food in your mouth, the epiglottis stands up to keep the windpipe open. This allows you to breathe while you are eating. When you swallow food, the epiglottis folds down. This closes off the windpipe. At the same time, another safety device—a piece of flexible tissue called the soft palate in the roof of the mouth—rises to block the nasal cavity. Once food enters the esophagus, the epiglottis and soft palate return to their normal positions. You can chew and breathe some more!

From your first bite until the last flush of the toilet, every piece of food you eat takes this journey through the digestive system.

SUPPORTING CAST: LIVER, PANCREAS, AND GALLBLADDER

Several other organs have important roles in the digestive process, particularly the liver, pancreas, and gallbladder. Many of the digestive juices and enzymes used throughout the digestive tract are produced or stored by these organs.

Once nutrients enter your blood, they travel to the liver. The liver is like a manufacturing plant that filters, processes, manufactures, and stores nutrients. The liver spends most of its time processing dissolved nutrients in the blood. It makes sure that the right nutrients are sent to the correct parts of the body. This organ also filters and flushes out toxic substances, such as pollutants, bacterial toxins, and chemicals from plants. Other cells in the liver remove bacteria, debris, and old red blood cells from the blood.

> Once the filtering is complete, the blood travels from the liver to the heart and lungs.

The liver also stockpiles nutrients, primarily vitamins, minerals, and glycogen. Glycogen is a form of stored glucose. When the body needs energy, the liver converts stored glycogen into glucose and sends it into the blood. The stored nutrients allow your body to survive without food for days and even weeks. The nutrients also serve as a backup in case your diet is missing a necessary nutrient.

FEED ME SOME NUTRIENTS

Can you name the six types of nutrients the human body needs to function properly? You may be disappointed to hear that it's not ice cream, candy, cheesecake, cake, pie, or cookies!

The nutrients your body needs to function are fats, proteins, carbohydrates, vitamins, minerals, and water.

During the digestive process, fats, proteins, and carbohydrates are broken down into smaller particles so they can be absorbed. Carbohydrates break down into sugars, which are the main energy source for the body and brain. Proteins break down into amino acids. They are used to build the main structures of cells. Fats break down into fatty acids. They are a stored source of energy for the body.

Vitamins, minerals, and water are absorbed directly through the gastrointestinal tract. About 65 percent of the body is made of water. Every time you sweat or breathe, your body loses water. That's why it's important to drink a lot of water. Vitamins are used for building tissues and structures in the body.

What happens if you do not eat enough nutrients? In the short term, probably not a lot. But in the long term, if your body does not get the nutrients it needs, body systems start to break down. In some cases, they can even fail.

Nutritional deficiencies can cause several health problems, including digestion problems, skin disorders, stunted bone growth, and dementia. One of the most common nutritional deficiencies in the world is iron deficiency.

BODY WISE

Vitamin C is used to build collagen, which is found in several types of tissue. Minerals are important for building bones, hair, skin, and blood cells. They also help turn food into energy.

VOCAB LAB

Write down what you think each word means. What root words can you find to help you? What does the context of the word tell you?

celiac disease, **esophagus**, **large intestine**, **nutrients**, **saliva**, **small intestine**, and **villi**.

Compare your definitions with those of your friends or classmates. Did you all come up with the same meanings? Turn to the text and glossary if you need help.

Feeling a little bit gassy? That's because of your gut microbes. Fermentation by gut microbes produces several different gases, including hydrogen, carbon dioxide, methane, and hydrogen sulfide. When a lot of gas is produced, you feel bloated and gassy. Foods that produce a lot of gas include corn, beans, and broccoli. If you're feeling more gassy than usual, it's probably because your gut microbes are working overtime!

Watch this video to learn more about microbes in your body.

 You are Your Microbes

When the body is too low on the mineral iron, it can lead to anemia, a blood disorder that causes fatigue, weakness, and other symptoms. So, eat your spinach and Brussels sprouts!

THERE'S *WHAT* IN MY GUT?

More than 100 trillion bacteria, viruses, and fungi live in your digestive tract. These microscopic organisms are the gut microbes. And you need them! Gut microbes provide the body with nutrients, help digestion, and defend against harmful microbes.

Microbes enter your body every day through your nose and mouth. They travel through the stomach and small intestine, where few remain because the environment is too acidic. The microbes that survive travel into the large intestine, where they help with digestion. About 70 percent of all gut microbes live in the large intestine where they digest what the body cannot. They use undigested carbohydrates for energy. They ferment fiber, which helps the body absorb minerals such as calcium and iron, and produce vitamins. Some microbes secrete vitamins, such as vitamin K.

Keeping healthy by eating plenty of nutrients is important to stay alive. For the body to make new life, the reproductive system steps in. We'll see how in the next chapter.

KEY QUESTIONS

- **How do the digestive system and the endocrine system work together?**
- **Why do you think some people continue to eat unhealthfully, even knowing that a good diet is important to their body?**

THE ROLE OF VILLI IN THE SMALL INTESTINE

As the digestive system breaks down food into simple molecules, the wall of the small intestine absorbs these molecules and moves them into the blood. Fingerlike projections called villi line the wall of the small intestine and aid in absorption. In this activity, you will see how the villi increase the small intestine's ability to absorb nutrients.

Ideas for Supplies ▼

- 4 cups with an equal amount of water
- graduated cylinder

- **Dip a single paper towel into the first cup of water.** Measure how much water it absorbed by squeezing the wet paper towel into the graduated cylinder.

- **Fold two paper towels together and dip them into the second cup of water.** Measure how much water they absorb. Repeat with three folded paper towels and four folded paper towels. Measure how much water is absorbed each time.

- **Which paper towel combination absorbed the most water?** Which absorbed the least? Explain why this occurred? How does this relate to the function of villi in the small intestine?

BODY WISE

Gut microbes also help protect the gut against harmful microbes. They fill the intestine walls and release substances that kill harmful bacteria.

To investigate more, does changing the way you fold the paper towels affect how much water they can absorb? Explain your results.

Ideas for Supplies ▼

- 1 uncoated aspirin tablet
- 1 enteric-coated aspirin tablet
- 2 clear plastic cups
- vinegar
- baking soda
- salt

To investigate more, test other forms of an over-the-counter medication, either with a different coating or in capsule form. Have an adult help you choose which medication to work with. How does the different form affect digestion? You could also try testing candy with different types of coatings. How do the coatings affect digestion?

DIGESTION OF COATED VS. NON-COATED ASPIRIN

While the digestion process works well for food, it is not always the best for medication. Some medications, such as aspirin, can be harsh on the stomach. To solve this problem, scientists have developed several different types of coating to prevent aspirin from being digested until it has passed from the stomach into the small intestine. In this activity, you will perform an experiment to test how these coatings work.

- **Fill a clear plastic cup with vinegar.** Fill a second clear plastic cup with a half cup of water, a pinch of salt, and 1½ teaspoons of baking soda.

- **Place both aspirin tablets into the cup with the vinegar.** The acidity of vinegar is similar to the acidity of the stomach's acids. What happens to each tablet?

- **After a few minutes, remove the coated tablet from the vinegar and put it in the second cup with the baking soda mixture, which mimics the small intestine.** What happens to the tablet? How long does it take for the entire tablet to dissolve?

- **How does this experiment model the digestive system?** Where in the body would you expect each tablet to dissolve and why? Why is this knowledge important to the development of new medications?

Chapter 8 ▶
Producing Life: The Reproductive System

How do humans reproduce?

When a male sex cell, or sperm, fertilizes a female sex cell, or egg, a fetus begins to develop. Eventually, a baby might be born to carry on the genes of their parents.

The ultimate biological goal of every living thing is to reproduce. Reproduction enables organisms to pass on their genetic material to offspring and ensures the survival of a species. Without reproduction, the species dies out and becomes extinct. In humans, the reproductive system contains all of the organs and glands that enable our species to create offspring.

Every cell in your body contains DNA from both your mother and your father. How did this happen? Each of your parents contributes half of the genetic material needed to create a new human. Together, they create a single cell that holds a full set of DNA instructions. That single cell starts its journey to become a baby—you!

A human's reproductive system creates specialized sex cells called gametes. Each gamete contains half of the genetic material in a normal human cell. During reproduction, a male's sex cell (sperm) combine with a female's sex cell (egg).

Unlike most other body systems, the reproductive system is different in males and females. Let's take a closer look at both male and female reproductive systems and how they work.

THE MALE REPRODUCTIVE SYSTEM

In males, the reproductive system includes glands, organs, and tubes that create, store, and deliver sperm out of the body and toward the female's egg. Two glands called the testicles, or testes, create sperm. This pair of oval-shaped glands are located outside of the body to keep the sperm at a cooler temperature than the human body. The scrotum, a pouch of thick skin and muscle, covers and protects the testes.

Extremely tiny, the male sperm looks a little bit like a tadpole. It has a head that carries a nucleus, which holds its DNA in 23 chromosomes. A tiny tail connects to the sperm head and gives it mobility to travel in a fluid. Small organs called the seminal vesicles produce the fluid that, when mixed with sperm, becomes semen.

> Sperm travel from the testes through a series of tubes on its way to meet a female egg.

Sperm travel in large groups, often more than 100 million. First, the sperm pass through a tightly coiled tube on top of each testicle called the epididymis. Next, the sperm continue through another tube called the vas deferens, which connects the epididymis to the urethra in the penis.

MEIOSIS

A normal human cell has 23 pairs of chromosomes for a full set of 46 chromosomes. To create reproductive cells that have only 23 chromosomes, a cell must undergo a special type of cell division, called meiosis. Remember, in mitosis, the cell's DNA makes a copy every time it forms a new cell. In meiosis, a single cell replicates and produces two daughter cells, each containing a full copy of the human genetic material. Next, the two daughter cells divide and produce a total of four granddaughter cells. The daughter cells' DNA does not replicate in this phase. Instead, it splits between the two granddaughter cells. The end result is four granddaughter cells that each hold 23 chromosomes, or half of the DNA of the original parent cell.

BODY WISE

When the scrotum senses cold temperature, it's smooth muscle contracts and pulls the scrotum and the testes closer to the body. This keeps sperm at the proper temperature.

The penis and the urethra have roles in both the urinary and reproductive systems. The male penis is made of muscles and tissue that fill with blood during the reproductive process. In the urinary system, the urethra is a tube that carries urine from the bladder through the penis to exit the body. The urethra also carries semen out of the body.

THE FEMALE REPRODUCTIVE SYSTEM

Inside the female body, a pair of organs called ovaries contain the female sex cells—they are called eggs, or ovum. The egg is so small, it can be seen only with a microscope. The female egg contains 23 chromosomes, which is half of the DNA in a human cell.

The ovaries do not make eggs—they store them. When a baby girl is born, her ovaries already hold all of the eggs that her body will make. Each egg, if fertilized with a male sperm, has the potential to grow and become a human baby.

In addition to storing eggs, the ovaries release hormones. When a female reaches puberty, the pituitary gland in the brain starts making hormones that stimulate the ovaries to make and release female sex hormones, such as estrogen. These hormones cause a female to develop breasts and menstruate. As a female matures, hormones cause the ovaries to release eggs as part of a monthly menstrual cycle.

When a woman becomes pregnant, the ovaries release hormones that enable the female body to grow and nurture a baby.

In a mature female, sex hormones trigger the ovaries to release an egg in a process called ovulation. This process occurs about once a month as part of the woman's menstrual cycle. Once the egg is released, finger-like extensions on the end of the fallopian tube catch it. Then, the egg travels through the fallopian tube until it reaches the uterus.

The uterus is a hollow, muscular organ located in the female pelvis. The walls of the uterus are made of muscle, which allows the uterus to change shape. When a woman is not pregnant, the uterus is about the size of a business card. When a woman is nine months pregnant, the uterus can stretch as large as a watermelon! Each month, the uterus builds a fluffy, blood-filled lining just in case a male sperm reaches a female egg and fertilizes it.

If the female egg meets a male sperm, it can be fertilized. Most of the time, this occurs in the fallopian tubes. The fertilized egg will implant itself in the blood-filled lining of the uterus. There, it might grow and develop into a baby.

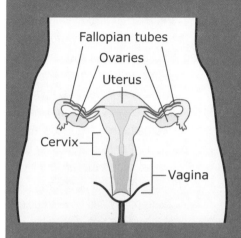

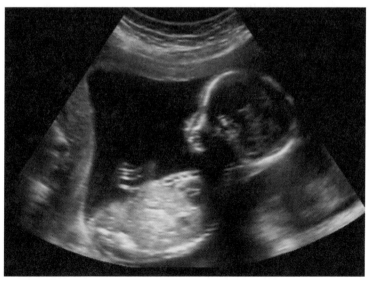

An ultrasound photograph of a fetus in the fourth month in the womb

BODY WISE

An unfertilized egg stays in the reproductive tract for about 12 to 24 hours after being released from the ovary.

Sometimes, couples struggle with infertility and have trouble reproducing. Infertility problems can affect both males and females. Some females do not ovulate regularly, so there is no egg for the sperm to fertilize. Other times, a woman's fallopian tubes may be blocked or their eggs may be too old. Males can have a low number of sperm or sperm that swim poorly and have trouble reaching the egg. There are a number of medical treatments for infertility. One treatment is called in vitro fertilization. In this treatment, doctors collect eggs from a woman and sperm from a man. They combine the male and female sex cells outside of the body in a lab to fertilize one or more of the eggs. They allow any fertilized eggs to develop for a short time outside the body into an embryo. Then, doctors implant the growing embryo into the woman's uterus, where it can continue to grow and develop into a baby.

If the woman's egg is not fertilized, the uterus does not need its blood-filled lining. It sheds the lining in a process called menstruation. Once shedding is complete, the uterus begins to build up a new lining.

When a baby is born, the muscles of the uterus contract to push the baby out of the uterus, through the vagina, and out of the body. The uterus connects to the vagina through a small opening called the cervix. The cervix's opening is very small, about the width of a straw. It expands during labor to allow a baby to pass from the uterus into the vagina. The vagina is a muscular, tunnel-like structure that connects the uterus to the outside of the body. Because the walls of the vagina are muscular, it can expand and contract to allow a baby to pass through it.

SEXUAL REPRODUCTION

Humans reproduce through a process called sexual reproduction. Sexual reproduction is an instinct, a natural pattern of behavior. We are born with the instinct to reproduce. Without reproduction and offspring, the human species would quickly die out.

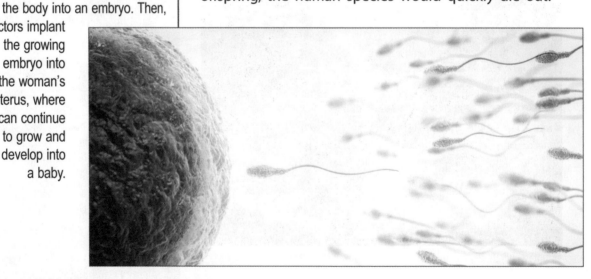

For many species, including humans, sexual reproduction involves a male and female parent. Each parent has their own sex cell—these are needed to create an offspring. Each sex cell holds half of the DNA needed for a human cell.

During sexual intercourse, the male releases sperm inside the female's vagina. Millions of tiny sperm swimming in semen travel in search of an egg. They swim from the vagina, through the cervix, and into the uterus. Only a few find their way into the upper fallopian tubes, where fertilization usually takes place. Sometimes, no sperm find an egg and they eventually die off. However, if a woman has ovulated and an egg is in the fallopian tubes, one of the sperm may find it. When the sperm finds the egg, it penetrates the egg's outer layer. Once this occurs, the egg hardens to prevent other sperm from penetrating it.

During fertilization, the sperm and egg combine to make a new offspring with a complete set of DNA. This single, combined cell is called a zygote. The zygote holds all of the DNA needed to create a baby.

> Within a few hours, the zygote begins to divide. It splits into two cells, then four cells, eight cells, and so on.

As it continues to divide and grow, the zygote travels down the fallopian tube to the uterus. The growing cluster of cells, now called a blastocyst, implants itself in the uterus's lining. There, it begins to grow and develop into a new human baby.

Now that you've explored all the different body systems, let's take a look at some of the things that threaten a healthy body and find out what you can do to stay safe and healthy!

BODY WISE

The uterus contains some of the strongest muscles in the female human body.

TEXT TO WORLD

Do you know any identical twins? Do some research to find out how they have the same genes!

KEY QUESTIONS

- **Why are the reproductive systems different for males and females?**
- **How is meiosis different from mitosis?**

Inquire & Investigate

CREATE A REPRODUCTIVE BOARD GAME

The reproductive system is one of the most important systems in the human body. This body system allows humans to reproduce and bear live offspring. Without the reproductive system, you would not be alive! Learning about the reproductive system can be fun. In this activity, you will create a board game to teach others about the reproductive system.

- **Gather the supplies that you will need to create your game board, game pieces, spinners, dice, questions cards, and any other pieces.** For example, you might use a poster board and markers to create a game board and small bits of clay to make game pieces.

- **When creating your board game, determine the objective of the game and the rules of play.** How will players move about the game board? What do they have to achieve during the game? How does a player win the game? The game should involve information about the reproductive system and how it works. You may need to do some research on the reproductive system as you create the game.

- **Once you have completed the game, play it with family or friends.** After playing, ask the players what they learned about the reproductive system from the game.

> **To investigate more,** what changes could you make to this board game so that you could use it to teach about other human body systems?

Chapter 9
Healthy Bodies

How does the body
avoid disease?

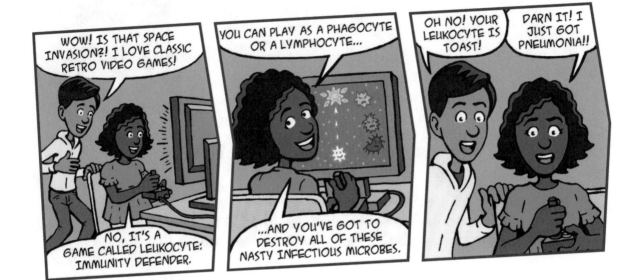

The body uses its own defensive methods to prevent sickness. You can help your body avoid illness with healthy practices such as washing hands and getting vaccinated.

So far, we've taken a close look at the different systems that make up your body and perform the work needed for you to move, think, react, reproduce, and generally function. In most people, all of these systems are robust and carry on with their work as long as the body is getting the nutrients it needs to maintain the energy required for the work. These systems also have help—they have a defense system!

Every day, germs and other microorganisms try to invade your body. At the same time, your body is constantly generating wastes that can become toxic to you. It might seem as though you're being attacked from both sides of your skin!

But your body has a plan to use its special systems—the skin, the immune system, and the urinary system—to keep out invaders and flush out wastes and toxins.

OUTER DEFENSE: YOUR SKIN

What's the largest organ in the body? Your skin! Skin has an essential role in keeping your body healthy. It is the first line of defense against the outside world. Skin acts as a barrier to protect you from physical damage, dehydration, and infection.

It provides a wall between your insides and the environment, including dangerous bacteria, and keeps your body sealed so the moisture you need doesn't simply evaporate from your systems. Your skin also regulates your body temperature by sweating when it needs to cool down and shivering when it needs to heat up.

Your skin has three layers: the epidermis, the dermis, and the hypodermis. The outer layer, the epidermis, is a self-renewing layer of cells. New cells are constantly formed at the base of the epidermis and travel up toward the skin's surface.

HEALTHY SWEAT

The skin is the body's largest excretory organ. Glands in the skin excrete sweat, a fluid that is mostly water but also contains salts and other waste products. Sweating is one way your body releases excess water and waste. It also helps to regulate your body temperature.

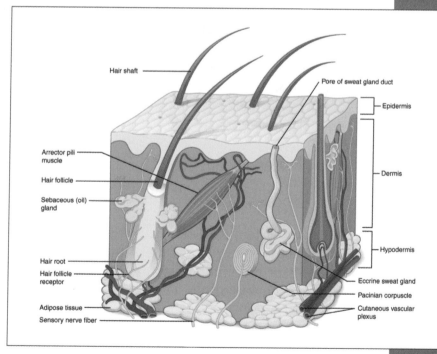

Hair shaft
Pore of sweat gland duct
Epidermis
Arrector pili muscle
Hair follicle
Sebaceous (oil) gland
Dermis
Hair root
Hair follicle receptor
Hypodermis
Adipose tissue
Sensory nerve fiber
Eccrine sweat gland
Pacinian corpuscle
Cutaneous vascular plexus

credit: Anatomy & Physiology, Connexions Website (CC BY 3.0)

As these new cells reach the surface, they fill with a tough protein called keratin and form a protective, outer layer. Each cell dies by the time it reaches the skin surface. The dead cells fall off and new ones rise to replace them.

Underneath the epidermis, the dermis is a thick middle layer that gives skin its strength and flexibility. The dermis holds the skin's nerve endings, hair roots, blood vessels, and sweat and oil glands.

The innermost layer of skin, the hypodermis, contains the body's stored fat cells that cushion the body and its organs, keep you warm, and supply energy when needed. The fat cells also store excess glucose as fatty acids.

BODY WISE

Because the epidermis sheds its cells, tattoos are inked on the skin's middle layer, the dermis, in order to be permanent. Because the epidermis is transparent, you can still see the tattoo.

The skin acts as a selectively permeable barrier. It allows some substances, such as drugs in a nicotine patch, sunblock cream, and antiseptic creams, to be absorbed and cross the barrier.

THE BODY'S DEFENSE SYSTEM

The immune system is your best defense against infectious organisms and other invaders. Many types of invaders can harm your body. Most invaders are tiny microbes, such as bacteria, viruses, fungi, and parasites. These tiny microbes hitch a ride into your body on food, water, or air. All these microbes can cause infections. Through a series of steps called the immune response, the immune system attacks invaders in the body that cause disease.

Invaders that attack the body
are also called antigens.

The immune system is made up of a network of cells, tissues, and organs. One of the main components of the immune system are white blood cells, also called leukocytes. Leukocytes seek out and destroy disease-causing invaders.

Many places in the body produce or store leukocytes, including the bone marrow, thymus, and spleen. The thymus and spleen are part of the lymphoid organs. Lymph nodes are small, bean-shaped nodes throughout the body—especially in your neck, armpits, and groin—that store leukocytes.

Leukocytes move between organs and nodes in your body using lymphatic vessels and blood vessels. In this way, the immune system patrols the body for germs or other harmful substances.

Two basic types of leukocytes work together: phagocytes and lymphocytes. Phagocytes are white blood cells that chew up invading organisms. Neutrophils are one type of phagocyte that primarily fight bacteria.

If your doctor thinks you might have a bacterial infection, they might order a blood test to see if you have an elevated number of neutrophils in your blood that have been triggered by the infection. Other phagocytes respond to specific types of invaders. Lymphocytes are cells that remember and recognize return invaders and help destroy them.

BODY WARS

There are two types of lymphocytes: B lymphocytes and T lymphocytes. B lymphocytes function as military intelligence. They travel around the body and seek out targets. When they find an antigen, they send signals to the T lymphocytes. The T lymphocytes are the immune system's first-line soldiers. They rush to the antigen and begin to destroy it. They are backed up by the phagocytes, which finish off the antigens.

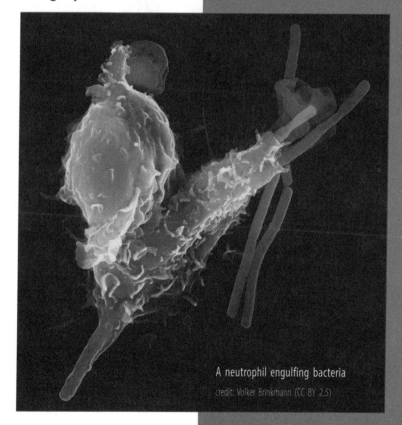

A neutrophil engulfing bacteria
credit: Volker Brinkmann (CC BY 2.5)

ANTIBODIES

The body is smart. It recognizes invaders that have tried to attack you before and remembers how to defeat them.

When antigens invade the body and are detected by the immune system, B lymphocytes produce specialized proteins that lock onto and tag specific antigens. These proteins are called antibodies. Antibodies are markers that signal T lymphocytes and phagocytes to attack the antigen.

Once produced, antibodies stay in the body. If the immune system detects a particular antigen again, the antibodies are ready to attack. That's why you only get sick once from certain diseases, such as chicken pox. Your immune system remembers the chicken pox antigen and deploys antibodies against it.

This is how immunizations work. When you are vaccinated for diseases such as chicken pox or measles, you receive a small amount of antigen. It's not enough antigen to make you sick, but it's enough to trigger your immune system to create antibodies that protect the body from a future attack by the antigen.

THREE TYPES OF IMMUNITY

All the protection that the immune system provides is called immunity. The human body has three types of immunity: innate, adaptive, and passive. You are born with innate immunity. It is a general type of protection for all humans.

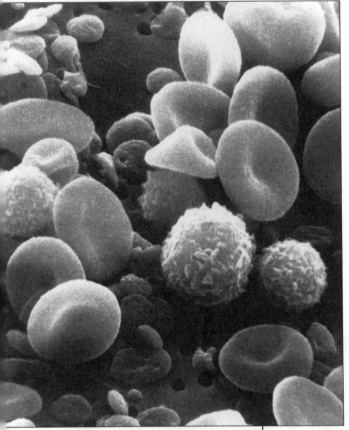

Human blood, including lymphocytes, a monocyte, a neutrophil, and many small disc-shaped platelets

credit: National Cancer Institute

BODY WISE

Innate immunity includes the body's external barriers, such as the skin and mucous membranes that line the nose, throat, and gastrointestinal tract.

Germs that harm other species don't affect humans because of innate immunity. For example, canine distemper is a serious disease in dogs. However, the virus that causes canine distemper doesn't affect humans, so we can't get this disease.

Another type of immunity, called adaptive or active immunity, develops throughout your life. Adaptive immunity develops as you are exposed to different diseases and produce antibodies to them.

> Adaptive immunity can also develop when you receive a vaccine against diseases.

It's very important to get vaccines, not only because you stay healthier but because your entire community stays healthier when fewer people are spreading diseases. In 2019, Portland, Oregon, experienced a surge in measles outbreaks when 73 people fell ill, many of them unvaccinated.

AGING IMMUNITY

As a person ages, their immune system has been exposed to more germs than a younger person and, as a result, has built up more immunity to different infections. That's why adults tend to get fewer colds than young children. However, in the elderly, the immune system doesn't work as well, which means older people are more susceptible to disease and often take longer to heal.

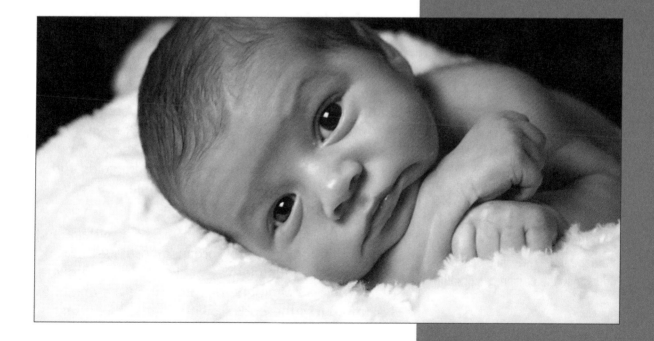

KIDNEY STONES

Sometimes, waste minerals build up in the kidneys, where they stick together and form a stone. Small kidney stones can pass out of the body without a problem. Other times, kidney stones are larger and more painful to pass. Sometimes, kidney stones become so large they become stuck somewhere in the urinary tract. If this causes an infection or other complications, surgery may be needed to remove the stone.

BODY WISE

When a person is having a severe allergic reaction, an EpiPen quickly delivers the drug epinephrine, which acts on the entire body to shut down the allergic response. Epinephrine constricts blood vessels, decreases swelling, relaxes the muscles around the airway, and opens the lungs so the person can breathe.

The third type of immunity, passive immunity, is borrowed from another source. Unlike innate and adaptive immunity, which last a lifetime, passive immunity lasts for only a short time. For example, babies receive antibodies from their mothers' milk that give the babies temporary immunity against diseases that the mothers are protected against. This helps to protect very young babies against infection before they are vaccinated.

IMMUNITY PROBLEMS

In most cases, the immune system works well to keep us healthy and to prevent infection. However, problems with the immune system can occur and can lead to infection and illness. Problems with the immune system fall into four main categories: immunodeficiency disorders, autoimmune disorders, allergic disorders, and cancers.

Immunodeficiency disorders occur when part of the immune system is not working properly or is missing entirely. Some people are born with these conditions. Other times, they occur because of infection or an interaction with a drug. For example, IgA deficiency is the most common immunodeficiency disorder. IgA is a type of antibody primarily found in the saliva and other body fluids that protect the body's entrances. If you have IgA deficiency, the body does not produce enough of the IgA antibody, so you often get more colds and respiratory infections than other people. You may also suffer from allergies.

Sometimes, the immune system makes a mistake and attacks the body's healthy organs and tissues. This causes an autoimmune disease. For example, lupus is a chronic autoimmune disease where the immune system attacks the body's own tissues and organs.

These attacks can cause inflammation that affects several body areas, such as the joints, skin, kidneys, blood cells, brain, heart, and lungs.

Some people can have an anaphylaxis reaction to wasp stings.

Did you know that allergies are a result of your immune system malfunctioning? Allergies occur when your immune system overreacts to substances that don't usually cause harm in the body, such as certain foods, pet hair, and pollen from plants.

The substances that cause the attacks are called allergens. The over-the-top immune response causes swelling, watery eyes, and sneezing. In some cases, it can even trigger a life-threatening reaction called anaphylaxis.

Anaphylaxis causes the immune system to release a flood of chemicals that cause your body to go into shock. Blood pressure drops rapidly and airways narrow, making it very difficult to breathe. You may also experience a rapid and weak pulse, skin rash, nausea, and vomiting. If not treated immediately, anaphylaxis can be fatal.

When cells in the immune system grow out of control, cancers occur. Leukemia occurs when leukocytes grow uncontrolled. Lymphoma is another type of immune system cancer.

Watch this video to learn about tuberculosis, the world's most infectious disease. Why are vaccines so important?

 TedEd TB

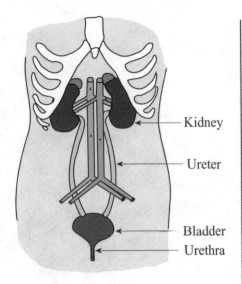

Kidney

Ureter

Bladder

Urethra

TAKING OUT THE TRASH

Who takes out the trash in your family? In the human body, that's the job of the urinary system. Passing urine is the body's way of taking out the trash. As the blood travels through the body, it picks up waste and excess nutrients. If left in the body, these could cause problems and even become life-threatening. The kidneys and the urinary system remove waste products and toxins from your body before they can do any harm.

When you drink a lot of water, what happens? You have to pee! You probably go to the bathroom several times a day without even thinking about how and why your body makes that happen. The urinary system is a network of organs that work together to make and get rid of urine. Urine contains salts, toxins, and water that need to be filtered out of the blood.

So, how does the urinary system work? The four main structures of the urinary system are the kidneys, ureters, bladder, and urethra. The kidneys are two bean-shaped organs located under your rib cage in the back, one on each side of the body. The adult kidney is about the size of a fist.

To make urine, blood travels to each kidney, where it flows through the nephrons, tiny filtering units that remove harmful substances from the blood. As the blood passes through a nephron, it flows through a tiny filter called a glomerulus. The filter removes excess water and other wastes from the blood but keeps blood cells and valuable proteins in the blood.

The fluid and substances filtered out of the blood travel down a tiny tube called a tubule. The tubule adjusts the level of salts, water, and wastes that will exit the body in urine.

The filtered blood leaves the kidney and flows back to the heart. From start to finish, it takes about five minutes for blood to pass through the kidneys.

Urine leaves the kidneys and travels through two long, muscular tubes called ureters to the bladder. Muscle contractions squeeze the urine along the ureter. That's why your bladder can fill even if you are lying down. As it fills with urine, the bladder expands. When it is full, nerves in the bladder wall send a message to the brain. This makes you feel like you have to pee.

When you go to the bathroom, the bladder walls tighten. The sphincter, a ring-like muscle that closes off the exit from the bladder to the urethra, relaxes. This allows urine to leave the bladder and pass through the urethra and exit the body.

The human body is an amazing machine. The body's many cells and tissues work together in complex organ systems. Each organ system, from the circulatory system to the digestive system, is in charge of specialized body functions, such as delivering oxygen to cells or breaking down food. Yet none of the body's systems operates alone. Each is connected to other body systems, communicating and giving each other instructions.

Together, they work to keep the body's complex machinery running smoothly. It's quite the balancing act, but one that your amazing body does each day!

KEY QUESTIONS

- **What can individuals do to keep all of their systems healthy and functioning?**
- **Why are vaccines important?**

BODY WISE

The average adult male can hold 17 fluid ounces in the bladder.

WASH YOUR HANDS!

One of the easiest ways to stay healthy is to wash your hands! Throughout the day, you touch people, objects, and surfaces and gather germs on your hands. If you touch your eyes, nose, or mouth with your hands, you can infect yourself with these germs. You can also spread the germs to other people. Washing your hands can limit the germs on your hands and their transfer to others. The best way to wash your hands is with soap and water, lathering well and scrubbing all surfaces of your hands and fingers for at least 20 seconds.

TEXT TO WORLD

Do you know people who refuse to be vaccinated? What are their reasons?

Ideas for Supplies ▼

- fine-grain sand
- food coloring
- water
- a tall, thin glass jar
- cheesecloth or filter paper

BODY WISE

Most people have two kidneys, but the human body can function with just one.

FILTERING WASTE

All organisms, including humans, must get rid of waste and toxins that build up in the body. In the human body, the primary organs that remove waste are the lungs, kidneys, and skin. The lungs get rid of carbon dioxide through exhalation. The skin excretes waste in sweat. The urinary system gets rid of waste in the body in the form of urine. In this activity, you can demonstrate how the kidneys work to filter waste out of the body.

- **Mix together 1 pound of sand, 1 gallon of water, and food coloring.** What does this represent?

- **Fill the jar about half full of water.** Place the filter paper or cheesecloth over the jar's top. Slowly pour the water and sand mixture through the filter paper or cheesecloth into the jar. What happens?

- **Remove the filter paper and pour out the water in the jar.** Add new water to the sand and water mixture and repeat pouring it into the filter-covered jar. Repeat several times. What happens to the sand and water mixture? How does this represent what the kidneys do?

> **To investigate more,** consider that when kidneys do not function properly, kidney disease and even kidney failure can occur. Choose a type of kidney problem and research it. How does the problem affect how the kidneys work? What effect does this have on the body? What happens if waste is not removed from the body? Design a model to demonstrate how this problem affects the kidneys.

SWEATY!

Everyone sweats—in fact, you need to sweat to stay healthy! But in many societies, sweat is seen as unclean. Some people spend a lot of money on products that prevent sweat or cover up the scent. In this activity, you will see how different types of antiperspirants work on the body's sweat.

- **Using a variety of antiperspirants, design an experiment to test the effectiveness of each type of antiperspirant.** Recruit athletic volunteers and have them perform exercises that make them sweat. Make sure that your experiment also includes a control group of volunteers for comparison.

- **Have the volunteers and the control group perform the same amount of exercise with and without the antiperspirant.** Measure and record the amount of sweat produced by each volunteer. You can measure the amount of sweat by comparing the sweat stains on a shirt, headband, other method. Make sure the conditions are similar for both exercise sessions— similar temperature, time of day, and humidity.

- **Create a graph or chart to present your measurements.** How did the antiperspirants affect the volunteers? Did some antiperspirants perform better than others? Why do you think this occurred? Did some antiperspirants perform better for the control group vs. the exercise group? Why do you think this occurred?

Inquire & Investigate

VOCAB LAB

Write down what you think each word means. What root words can you find to help you? What does the context of the word tell you?

antibodies, autoimmune disorder, bladder, epidermis, immunity, immunodeficiency disorder, lymph nodes, ureter, and **urethra.**

Compare your definitions with those of your friends or classmates. Did you all come up with the same meanings? Turn to the text and glossary if you need help.

To investigate more, perform a similar experiment dividing the volunteers by age or gender. Does this affect your results? Why or why not?

GLOSSARY

abdominal cavity: the cavity within the abdomen between the abdominal wall and the spine.

abdominalpelvic cavity: a body cavity that consists of the abdominal cavity and the pelvic cavity.

action potential: occurs when a neuron sends information down an axon, away from the cell body.

active transport: the movement of molecules across a cell membrane into a region of higher concentration, which requires energy.

adapt: to adjust to new conditions.

adaptive immunity: immunity that develops as a person is exposed to diseases and vaccines.

adenosine triphosphate (ATP): chemical energy that provides energy for cellular work.

adipose: fat-storage tissue.

adrenal glands: endocrine glands that produce a variety of hormones, including adrenaline and cortisol.

allergen: something that triggers an allergic reaction.

allergies: an immune response by the body to a substance or food to which it has become hypersensitive.

altitude: height above sea level.

alveoli: the tiny air sacs in the lungs where the exchange of oxygen and carbon dioxide takes place. Singular is alveolus.

amino acid: an organic compound that serves as a building block for proteins.

anaphylaxis: a reaction to an antigen that causes life-threatening symptoms such as welts, difficulty in breathing, and shock.

anatomy: the science of the structure of living things.

anemia: a blood disorder in which a person does not have enough healthy red blood cells to carry enough oxygen to the body.

angina: chest pain caused by reduced blood flow to the heart.

anterior: front or ventral.

antibodies: proteins that help the immune system fight infections or bacteria.

antigen: a foreign molecule on a virus or bacterium that invades your body.

aorta: the large artery carrying oxygenated blood from the heart.

appendage: a body part that sticks out from the main body, such as an arm or leg.

appendicular region: the body's appendages.

arrhythmia: a heartbeat that is too fast, too slow, or irregular.

arteriole: a small branch of an artery.

artery: a blood vessel that carries oxygenated blood away from the heart.

asthma: a respiratory condition marked by spasms in the bronchi of the lungs, causing difficulty in breathing.

atrium: one of the two upper chambers of the heart. Plural is atria.

autoimmune disorder: a disease in which the body's immune system attacks its own tissues and cells.

autonomic system: the part of the peripheral nervous system that regulates the function of internal organs such as the heart, stomach, and intestines.

axial region: everything down the center axis of the body.

axon terminal: the end of an axon that fires an electrical signal across a synapse to another neuron.

axon: a fiber-like extension of a neuron that carries electrical signals to other neurons.

B lymphocyte: a type of white blood cell that produces antibodies.

bacteria: single-celled prokaryotic organisms found in soil, water, plants, and animals. They help decay food, and some bacteria are harmful. Singular is bacterium.

ball-and-socket joint: a joint, such as the hip joint, where the ball-like end of one bone fits into a curved depression in another bone, allowing movement in all directions.

bile: a fluid produced by the liver that aids in digestion.

bladder: a sac-like organ that holds urine until it is excreted from the body.

blastocyst: a growing cluster of cells that implants in the female uterus and will develop into a human baby.

blood pressure: the pressure exerted by circulating blood on the walls of blood vessels.

body cavity: a space that holds internal organs.

body system: a group of organs and tissues that work together to perform a specific function.

bone: hard, connective tissue in an animal's body that provides support, protection, and a place for muscle attachment.

bone marrow: the fatty tissue inside bone cavities that makes red and white blood cells.

brain stem: the lower part of the brain that connects to the spinal cord, responsible for basic life-support functions.

brain: the organ that serves as the center of the body's nervous system.

bronchiole: a tiny branch of a bronchus.

bronchus: an air passage from the trachea to a lung. Plural is bronchi.

calcium: a mineral found mainly in the hard part of bones.

cancellous bone: the spongy tissue that makes up the inside of bone.

capillaries: tiny blood vessels that connect the smallest arteries with the smallest veins and deliver oxygen and nutrients to the body's tissues.

carbohydrate: an important source of energy found in the sugars, starches, and fibers in fruits, grains, vegetables, and milk products.

carbon dioxide: a combination of carbon and oxygen that is formed by the burning of fossil fuels, the rotting of plants and animals, and the breathing out of animals or humans.

cardiac muscle: muscle tissue found in the heart.

cardiovascular system: the body system that includes the heart and blood vessels. Also called the circulatory system.

cartilage: a tough, fibrous connective tissue.

cell: the smallest unit of life.

central nervous system (CNS): the brain and spinal cord.

cerebellum: the area of the brain located behind the cerebrum that helps regulate posture, balance, and coordination.

cerebral cortex: the outer, wrinkled part of the brain, where most higher-level processing occurs.

cerebrum: the largest part of the brain, where most higher-level functions and processing occur.

cervix: a cylinder-shaped neck of tissue that connects the vagina and uterus.

chamber: one of four sections of the heart that are hollow and receive and pump out blood.

chromosomes: parts of a cell that contain genes, which are what determine a person's physical characteristics.

cilia: small, hairlike projections on the outer surfaces of some cells.

circadian rhythm: the body's 24-hour sleep-wake-eat cycle.

clot: a lump made by a substance such as blood getting thicker and sticking together.

collagen: a protein that provides a soft framework for bone.

comparative anatomy: the study of the similarities and differences in the structures of different species.

concentration: the amount of a substance in a specified area or volume.

connective tissue: the tendons, ligaments, and joint capsules that connect bones with bones and muscles with bones to provide support for the skeleton and allow it to move.

contract: to decrease in size.

coronary: relating to the heart.

corpus callosum: a thick band of nerve tissue that connects the right and left hemispheres of the brain and sends messages between them.

cortical bone: the hard outer layer of bone.

cortisol: a hormone produced in response to stress.

cranial: relating to the skull.

cranial cavity: the cavity inside the skull that holds the brain.

cytoplasm: the jelly-like fluid inside a cell.

cytoskeleton: the meshwork of proteins connecting to every organelle and every part of the cell membrane.

dehydration: the dangerous loss of body fluids.

dementia: a group of brain diseases that cause the gradual decline in a person's ability to think and remember.

dendrite: a branch on a neuron that receives messages from other neurons and delivers them to the main body of the nerve cell.

dermis: the thick layer of the skin below the epidermis.

developmental anatomy: the study of the life cycle of the human body and how body parts change during a person's lifespan.

diaphragm: the muscle that separates the chest from the abdomen.

diastole: the passive rhythmical expansion or dilation of the cavities of the heart during which they fill with blood.

differentiate: to make different through development or design.

diffusion: the movement of substances from an area of higher concentration to an area of lower concentration until the distribution is equal.

digestive system: the body system that breaks down food to release essential nutrients to fuel the body.

dilate: to open or expand.

dissect: to methodically cut up a body after death to study the insides.

distal: farther from the point of attachment or the body's trunk.

DNA: deoxyribonucleic nucleic acid. Genetic material that contains instructions that make us who we are.

dorsal cavity: found on the posterior of the body and includes the cranial cavity, which holds the brain, and the spinal cavity, which holds the spinal cord.

electron microscope: a type of microscope that uses a beam of electrons to create an image of the specimen.

embryo: an organism at its early stages of development.

emotion: a strong feeling about something or someone.

endocardium: a thin membrane lining the cavities of the heart.

endocrine system: a group of glands that produce hormones that regulate many processes in the body.

endocytosis: a process that moves a molecule into a cell.

endoplasmic reticulum: a network of membranes that makes changes and transports materials through a cell.

enteric nervous system: the part of the nervous system that helps the body with the process of digestion.

enzyme: a chemical in living things that speeds up or slows down reactions.

epicardium: the inner layer of the pericardium that closely envelops the heart.

epidermis: the outer layer of the skin.

GLOSSARY

epididymis: a tightly coiled tube on top of the testicle through which sperm travel.

epinephrine: a hormone produced in high-stress situations. Also called adrenaline.

epithelial tissue: a type of tissue that is used for coverings and linings in the body.

equilibrium: balance.

esophagus: a muscular tube that transports food from the mouth and pharynx to the stomach.

eukaryotic cell: a cell with a nucleus.

exocytosis: a process that moves a molecule out of cell.

fallopian tubes: a pair of tubes that carry the female egg from the ovary to the uterus.

fascicle: a bundle of muscle fibers.

feedback loop: the path by which some of the output of a body system is returned to the input.

fiber: a strand of tissue, such a nerve fiber, muscle fiber, or connective fiber.

filtration: passing liquid through a filter to clean it of particles.

flat bone: a type of bone that is flat and functions to protect internal organs and provide an attachment site for muscles.

friction: the rubbing of one object against another.

frontal plane: the plane that divides the body into the front and back.

gallbladder: an organ in the digestive system that stores bile produced by the liver.

gamete: a sex cell such as an egg or a sperm that contains half of an organism's DNA and combines with another gamete during sexual reproduction.

gastric: related to the stomach.

gene: a section of DNA that codes for a particular trait.

genetic: relating to genes, which are units of DNA and RNA that assign organisms their characteristics.

germ: a microscopic organism that can cause harm.

gland: an organ in the human body that secretes particular chemical substances for use in the body.

glucose: a sugar that is a major source of energy for cells.

gluten: a substance found in certain cereals, especially wheat, that causes illness in people with celiac disease.

Golgi apparatus: a packaging organelle in a cell.

gravity: a force that pulls all objects toward the earth.

groin: the area of the body above the thighs.

gross anatomy: the study of the large parts of the body.

hemisphere: either of the two halves of the brain.

hemoglobin: a substance in red blood cells that combines with and carries oxygen around the body and gives blood its red color.

hinge joint: a joint, such as the elbow or knee, that permits movement in only one direction.

histologic anatomy: the study of the different types of tissue throughout the body and the cells.

homeostasis: the state of the human body being in balance.

hormone: a chemical messenger that regulates the activity of cells.

humerus: the upper arm bone.

hypodermis: the innermost layer of skin.

hypothalamus: an area of the brain that produces hormones that control many body functions, including hunger, thirst, mood, and emotion.

immune system: the network of cells in your body that fight invading cells.

immunity: the body's ability to withstand harmful invaders such as bacteria, viruses, fungi, and other foreign bodies.

immunization: exposing a person to a tiny dose of a disease to make the person resistant to it.

immunodeficiency disorder: a disorder that occurs when the immune system is not working properly or is missing entirely.

in vitro fertilization: a medical procedure whereby an egg is fertilized by sperm in a test tube or elsewhere outside the body.

infection: illness caused by a bacteria or virus.

inferior: below or lower than another body part.

inferior vena cava: a large vein that carries blood from the middle and lower parts of the body into the heart.

infertility: the inability to have children.

inflammation: part of the complex biological response of body tissues to harmful stimuli, such as pathogens, damaged cells, or irritants. It is a protective response.

innate immunity: immunity that a person is born with.

insertion point: the place where one end of a skeletal muscle is attached to a bone that moves when the muscle contracts.

insulin: a hormone produced in the pancreas that regulates the amount of glucose in the blood.

interneuron: a neuron that communicates between sensory and motor neurons.

involuntary muscle: a smooth muscle that contracts without a person thinking about it.

irregular bone: a bone that doesn't fit in another category. The vertebrae in the spine are irregular bones.

joint capsule: an envelope surrounding a synovial joint.

joint: the point where two bones meet and move relative to one another.

keratin: a protein that makes up the tough part of your skin.

kidney: an organ in the urinary system that filters the blood and produces urine to carry waste products out of the body.

lactic acid: an acid produced in the muscle cells and red blood cells when the body breaks down carbohydrates to use for energy and oxygen levels are low.

lactose intolerance: the inability to digest the protein lactose, which is often found in dairy products.

large intestine: the part of the digestive system that connects the small intestine to the rectum.

larynx: the organ that produces sound in the human body, also known as the voice box.

lateral: on the side.

leukemia: a type of blood cancer in which white blood cells called leukocytes grow uncontrolled.

leukocyte: a type of white blood cell.

ligament: a tissue that connects and holds bones together.

lipid: a key substance in most cell membranes that doesn't mix well with water. Includes fats, oils, sterols, and other fatty acids.

liver: an organ that cleans the blood and has an important role in digestion.

long bone: a bone that is longer than it is wide and functions to support body weight and facilitate movement.

lungs: a pair of organs located within the chest that remove carbon dioxide from and bring oxygen to the blood and are part of the respiratory system.

lymph node: a small structure that is part of the body's immune system.

lymphocyte: a type of white blood cell.

lysosome: an organelle in the cytoplasm of eukaryotic cells that holds enzymes.

magnetic resonance imaging (MRI): a form of medical imaging that uses high-frequency radio waves and a strong magnetic field.

marrow: a soft substance inside bones where blood cells are produced.

mature: fully developed.

medial: toward the middle of the body.

meiosis: a type of cell division that results in four daughter cells, each with half the number of chromosomes of the parent cell.

melatonin: a hormone released by the pineal gland that makes a person sleepy.

membrane: a thin covering.

menstruate: the monthly shedding of the uterus lining when a woman is not pregnant.

metabolism: a set of chemical reactions within the cells of living things that allows them to grow, reproduce, maintain their structure, and respond to the environment.

microbe: a living thing too small to be seen without a microscope. Also called a microorganism.

microorganism: a microscopic organism such as a bacterium, virus, or fungus.

mitochondria: organelles within a cell that produce energy.

mitosis: the process of cell division.

molecule: a unit of matter consisting of two or more atoms.

motor neuron: a neuron that activates the muscles.

mucus: a thick fluid found in the respiratory, digestive, reproductive, and urinary systems.

muscle: a tissue that contains cells called fibers that contract and can convert chemical energy into mechanical energy.

musculoskeletal: relating to the muscles and skeletal system.

nephron: a tiny filtering unit in the kidneys that removes harmful substances from the blood.

nerve impulse: a signal transmitted along a nerve fiber.

nerve: a living fiber that carries information between the brain and the rest of the body.

nervous system: the parts of the body that receive and interpret stimuli and send responses.

nervous tissue: groups of organized cells in the nervous system.

neuron: a special cell that sends electrical and chemical messages to the brain.

neurotransmitter: a chemical secreted by neurons that carries signals across a synapse to another neuron.

neutrophil: a white blood cell that cleans a wound.

nuclear envelope: the membrane that surrounds a cell's nucleus.

nucleus: the central part of a cell that controls how it functions. Plural is nuclei.

nutrients: the substances in food that living things need to live and grow.

optic nerve: the part of the eye that sends messages from the retina to the brain.

organ: a part of an organism that is self-contained and has a specific vital function, such as the heart or liver in humans.

organelle: a structure within a cell that has a special function.

organism: a living thing, such as a plant or animal.

origin point: the place where one end of a voluntary muscle is attached to a bone that remains relatively fixed.

osmosis: a process by which molecules tend to pass through a semi-permeable membrane from an area of higher concentration.

ossification: the process of forming and hardening new bone tissue.

osteoblast: a cell involved in bone formation.

osteoclast: a cell that dissolves and resorbs old bone tissue.

ovary: an organ in the female reproductive system that holds eggs.

oxygen: a gas in the air that people and animals need to breathe to stay alive.

oxygenated: filled with oxygen.

oxytocin: a hormone that makes you happy when you interact with people you like.

GLOSSARY

pancreas: a large gland behind the stomach that secretes digestive enzymes.

parasympathetic nervous system: one part of the autonomic nervous system that returns the body to its normal resting state after it encounters a threat.

parathyroid gland: a gland that regulates calcium, located behind the thyroid gland in the neck.

passive immunity: immunity borrowed from another source that lasts only a short time.

passive transport: the movement of molecules across cell membranes without using energy.

pelvic cavity: a body cavity surrounded by the bones of the pelvis.

pelvis: the large bony structure near the end of a vertebrate's backbone where the legs attach.

pericardial cavity: a space between the two layers of the pericardium around the heart.

pericardium: the membrane that surrounds the heart.

peripheral nervous system (PNS): the part of the nervous system that includes all of the nerves and neurons outside the brain and spinal cord.

peroxisome: a small organelle in many cells that contains digestive enzymes.

pH: a measure of whether something is acidic or basic.

phagocyte: a white blood cell that destroys invading cells.

physiology: the study of the internal workings of living organisms.

pituitary gland: a major gland in the endocrine system that produces hormones that control other glands and many body functions.

pivot joint: a type of joint that allows side-to-side movement, such as the joint at the top of the spine that allows the head to pivot.

plane: a two-dimensional, flat surface with no thickness.

plaque: fatty deposits on artery walls.

plasma: the colorless fluid part of blood.

platelet: a tiny, flat cell fragment in the blood that helps blood clot.

pleural cavity: the body cavity that holds the lungs and separates them from the chest walls.

pneumonia: an infection in the lower respiratory system.

posterior: the back of something.

prokaryotic cell: a simple, single-celled organism without a nucleus.

protein synthesis: the process of building a protein.

protein: a nutrient that is essential to the growth and repair of tissue.

protrusion: something that sticks out.

proximal: near the point of attachment or the body's trunk.

pulmonary artery: the artery that carries blood from the heart to the lungs.

pulmonary vein: the vein that carries blood from the lungs to the heart.

reasoning: the process of thinking about something in an intelligent way in order to make a decision or form an opinion.

receptor: a structure that receives stimuli and produces a nerve impulse to send information.

rectum: a chamber that begins at the end of the large intestine and ends at the anus.

red blood cell: a blood cell that contains hemoglobin, which allows it to carry oxygen and carbon dioxide through the bloodstream.

reflex action: an involuntary and often instantaneous movement in response to a stimulus.

region: a specific area of the body.

remodel: to remove mature bone tissue from the skeleton and form new bone tissue.

reproduction: making something new, just like itself.

respiratory system: the body system having to do with breathing. It includes the lungs.

ribosome: the protein-making factory in a cell.

RNA: the acronym for ribonucleic acid. RNA is genetic material that contains the code to make a certain protein.

sagittal plane: the division of the body or organ lengthwise into right and left sides.

saliva: a fluid produced by the salivary glands in the mouth that helps to break down food.

scrotum: a pouch of skin that holds a man's testicles.

secrete: to produce a liquid.

semen: the male reproductive fluid that contains sperm cells.

semi-permeable: a membrane that allows certain substances to pass through but not others.

seminal vesicles: a pair of glands in the male reproductive system that secrete semen.

sensory neuron: a neuron that converts external stimuli from the environment into internal electrical impulses.

sensory receptor: a specialized neuron in the sense organs that detects stimuli and sends messages to the brain.

serotonin: a neurotransmitter that makes you alert and responds to light levels.

sesamoid bone: a small bone embedded in a tendon or a muscle.

short bone: a small bone shaped like a cube that provides stability while still allowing for movement.

skeletal muscle: a muscle that is attached to a bone by tendons and is responsible for movement. Also known as a voluntary muscle.

skeleton: the framework of bones that supports the body.

skull: the bony framework of the head that protects the brain.

small intestine: the part of the digestive system that is a long thin tube that winds and snakes around the lower abdomen and connects the stomach to the large intestine.

smooth muscle: an involuntary muscle that cannot be consciously controlled. Smooth muscle often lines the body's organs.

soft palate: the fleshy, flexible part toward the back of the roof of the mouth.

soma: the body of a neuron.

somatic system: the part of the peripheral nervous system that carries sensory and motor information to and from the central nervous system.

sound wave: an invisible vibration in the air that you hear as sound.

species: a group of similar organisms that can reproduce with each other and produce fertile offspring.

sperm: the cell that comes from a male in the reproductive process.

sphincter: a round muscle that opens and closes to let something pass through.

spinal cavity: the body cavity that holds the spinal cord within the vertebrae.

spinal cord: a thick cord of nerve tissue that links the brain to nerves in the rest of the body.

spleen: an organ that filters the blood.

sternum: the wide, flat bone that joins your ribs together in front, also called the breastbone.

stimulus: a change in an organism's environment that causes an action, activity, or response. Plural is stimuli.

striated: having a striped appearance.

stroke: a lack of oxygen to part of the brain caused by the blocking or breaking of a blood vessel.

superficial: near the surface of the body.

superior: higher or above another body part.

superior vena cava: a large vein that carries blood from the upper half of the body and returns it to the heart.

suprachiasmatic nucleus (SCN): a tiny area of the hypothalamus in the brain that controls the body's circadian rhythm.

sympathetic nervous system: a part of the autonomic nervous system that prepares the body to respond to a threat.

synapse: a gap between two neurons through which communication occurs.

synovial joint: a joint that has a space between two bones and is filled with cushioning synovial fluid.

systole: the part of the heartbeat when the heart muscle contracts and pumps blood from the chambers into the arteries.

T lymphocyte: a type of white blood cell that attacks foreign invaders in the body.

technology: the tools, methods, and systems used to solve a problem or do work.

tendon: a tissue that connects muscles to bones.

testicles: the two oval organs that produce sperm cells in the male reproductive system.

thoracic: relating to the area of the body between the base of the neck and the abdomen.

thoracic cavity: the body cavity between the base of the neck and the abdomen that holds the trachea, bronchi, lungs, esophagus, heart, and several major blood vessels.

thrombocyte: a platelet.

thymus: a gland that produces T cells for the immune system.

thyroid: a large gland in the neck that secretes hormones regulating growth and development through the rate of metabolism.

tissue: a group or mass of similar cells working together to perform common functions.

trachea: a tube in the neck that extends from the larynx to the bronchi and acts as a passageway for air.

transverse plane: the division of a body or organ horizontally into superior (top) and inferior (bottom) sections.

tuberculosis (TB): a deadly disease of the lungs.

tubule: a small tube-like structure.

tumor: a growth or group of cancer cells.

ureter: a long muscular tube that connects the kidneys to the bladder.

urethra: a long tube from which urine exits the body.

urine: a fluid made up of waste materials that need to be removed from the body. Urine is excreted from the body through the urethra.

uterus: part of the female reproductive system in which a baby develops.

valve: a structure that controls the passage of fluid through a tube.

vas deferens: a duct in the male reproductive system through which sperm cells travel from the testicles to the urethra.

vein: a blood vessel that carries blood back to the heart.

vena cava: a main vein into the heart.

ventral cavity: a cavity located on the anterior of the body that holds many organs.

ventricle: one of the two lower chambers of the heart that pump blood out of the heart.

venule: a very small vein.

vertebrae: the bones that make up the spinal column.

vesicle: a small fluid-filled sac within the body.

villi: fingerlike projections on the wall of the small intestine that aid in absorption of nutrients.

virus: a non-living microbe that can cause disease.

vocal cords: two tiny ridges that lie across the larynx and open and close to make sounds.

white blood cell: a cell that protects against infection by destroying diseased cells and germs.

X-ray: a technology that uses radiation to allow doctors to see bones inside a body.

RESOURCES

BOOKS

Patricia Daniels, Christina Wilsdon, and Jen Agresta. *Ultimate Bodypedia: An Amazing Inside-Out Tour of the Human Body*. National Geographic, 2014.

How the Body Works: The Facts Simply Explained. DK Publishing, 2016.

Kevin Langford. *The Everything Guide to Anatomy and Physiology: All You Need to Know About How the Human Body Works*. Adams Media, 2015.

Carla Mooney. *The Brain: Journey Through the Universe Inside Your Head*. Nomad Press, 2015.

Carla Mooney. *Human Movement: How the Body Walks, Runs, Jumps, and Kicks*. Nomad Press, 2017.

Alice Roberts. *The Complete Human Body*. DK Publishing, 2016.

Laura Willis. *Anatomy & Physiology Made Incredibly Easy!* Wolters Kluwer, 2017.

WEBSITES

Biology 4 Kids—Systems:
biology4kids.com/files/systems_main.html

Body Basics Library:
kidshealth.org/en/teens/your
-body/?WT.ac=t-nav-your-body

Get Body Smart:
getbodysmart.com

The Human Body: Anatomy, Facts & Functions:
livescience.com/37009-human-body.html

The Human Body:
healthline.com/human-body-maps

National Geographic: The Human Body:
nationalgeographic.com/science/health
-and-human-body/human-body

METRIC CONVERSIONS

Use this chart to find the metric equivalents to the English measurements in this activity. If you need to know a half measurement, divide by two. If you need to know twice the measurement, multiply by two.

ENGLISH	METRIC	
1 inch	2.5	centimeters
1 foot	30.5	centimeters
1 yard	0.9	meter
1 mile	1.6	kilometers
1 pound	0.5	kilogram
1 teaspoon	5	milliliters
1 tablespoon	15	milliliters
1 cup	237	milliliters

SELECTED BIBLIOGRAPHY

"Anatomy & Physiology," SEER Training Modules, National Cancer Institute.
training.seer.cancer.gov/anatomy

"How the Heart Works," National Heart, Lung, and Blood Institute.
nhlbi.nih.gov/health-topics/how-heart-works

"How the Lungs Work," National Heart, Lung, and Blood Institute.
nhlbi.nih.gov/health-topics/how-lungs-work

"Inside the Cell," National Institute of General Medical Sciences. 2005.

"Overview of the Immune System," National Institute of Allergy and Infectious Disease.
niaid.nih.gov/research/immune-system-overview

The Complete Human Body by Dr. Alice Roberts, DK Publishing, 2016.

"Your Digestive System and How It Works," National Institute of Diabetes and Digestive and Kidney Diseases.
niddk.nih.gov/health-information/digestive-diseases/digestive-system-how-it-works#whyis

QR CODE GLOSSARY

page 8: youtube.com/watch?v=pQUMJ6Gh9Bw

page 14: youtube.com/watch?v=C6hn3sA0ip0

page 17: youtube.com/watch?v=URUJD5NEXC8

page 24: youtube.com/watch?v=ndDkPLNVNN8

page 28: youtube.com/watch?v=jqy0i1KXUO4

page 38: youtube.com/watch?v=tzCIE1weHrU

page 45: youtube.com/watch?v=CWFyxn0qDEU

page 52: youtube.com/watch?v=mZvzl8KH6iI

page 61: news-medical.net/health/What-is-the-Nervous-System.aspx

page 63: faculty.washington.edu/chudler/split.html

page 66: ed.ted.com/lessons/the-mysterious-science-of-pain-joshua-w-pate

page 67: scienceweek.net.au/neural-knitworks/neuron-gallery

page 77: youtube.com/watch?v=eWHH9je2zG4

page 83: youtube.com/watch?v=l7FPkyOtnTg

page 86: ed.ted.com/lessons/you-are-your-microbes-jessica-green-and-karen-guillemin

page 105: ed.ted.com/lessons/what-makes-tb-the-world-s-most-infectious-killer-melvin-sanicas

INDEX

INDEX